BIBLE
Promise
Book®

*500 Scriptures
to Grow
Your Faith*

The
BIBLE
Promise
Book ®

500 Scriptures
to Grow
Your Faith

Written and Compiled by
Deborah D. Cole

BARBOUR BOOKS
An Imprint of Barbour Publishing, Inc.

ISBN 978-1-64352-114-5

Scripture quotations are taken from the King James Version of the Bible.

Published by Barbour Books, an imprint of Barbour Publishing, 1810 Barbour Drive, Uhrichsville, Ohio 44683, www.barbourbooks.com

Our mission is to inspire the world with the life-changing message of the Bible.

 Member of the
Evangelical Christian
Publishers Association

CONTENTS

ARMOR OF GOD

Father, thank You for the safety and security You provide. When You adopted me into Your family, You gave me a suit of spiritual armor. No matter how dangerous this world may be, You are bigger and stronger and overflowing with love for Your children. . .for me. Help me, Lord, to put on Your armor daily and to run to Your side as the ultimate shelter. I know I am physically secure until the moment You decide to call me home—and in Jesus I am spiritually secure forever. Thank You, Father, that nothing will separate me from Your love!

1.

And Elisha prayed, and said, Lord, I pray thee, open his eyes, that he may see. And the Lord opened the eyes of the young man; and he saw: and, behold, the mountain was full of horses and chariots of fire round about Elisha.

2 Kings 6:17

2.

For thou hast been a shelter for me,
and a strong tower from the enemy.

PSALM 61:3

———

3.

He shall cover thee with his feathers,
and under his wings shalt thou trust:
his truth shall be thy shield and buckler.

PSALM 91:4

———

4.

As the mountains are round about Jerusalem,
so the LORD is round about his people
from henceforth even for ever.

PSALM 125:2

5.

The name of the LORD is a strong tower:
the righteous runneth into it, and is safe.

PROVERBS 18:10

6.

He put on righteousness as a breastplate,
and an helmet of salvation upon his head;
and he put on the garments of vengeance for
clothing, and was clad with zeal as a cloak.

ISAIAH 59:17

7.

The night is far spent, the day is at hand:
let us therefore cast off the works of darkness,
and let us put on the armour of light.

ROMANS 13:12

8.

Put on the whole armour of God, that ye may be able to stand against the wiles of the devil.

EPHESIANS 6:11

9.

Stand therefore, having your loins girt about with truth, and having on the breastplate of righteousness; and your feet shod with the preparation of the gospel of peace; above all, taking the shield of faith, wherewith ye shall be able to quench all the fiery darts of the wicked. And take the helmet of salvation, and the sword of the Spirit, which is the word of God.

EPHESIANS 6:14–17

10.

But let us, who are of the day, be sober, putting on the breastplate of faith and love; and for an helmet, the hope of salvation.

1 THESSALONIANS 5:8

ASSURANCE OF SALVATION

Thank You, Lord, for saving me. I may not always feel as if I am saved, but I know—truly know—that I am because Your Word assures me of it. You alone are the one who knows me as I am, and You alone know how much I needed salvation. Through Your death You have saved me, and by Your blood I no longer carry the guilt of my sin. You reach out to me, and I reach out to You. You hear me. You listen to me. You speak to my heart and welcome me into Your arms. I am Yours, for now and for always. Amen.

11.

Truly my soul waiteth upon God: from him cometh my salvation. He only is my rock and my salvation; he is my defence: I shall not be greatly moved.

PSALM 62:1–2

12.

For God hath not appointed us to wrath, but to obtain salvation by our Lord Jesus Christ, who died for us, that, whether we wake or sleep, we should live together with him. Wherefore comfort yourselves together, and edify one another, even as also ye do.

1 THESSALONIANS 5:9–11

13.

And ye shall be hated of all men for my name's sake: but he that endureth to the end shall be saved.

MATTHEW 10:22

14.

He that believeth and is baptized shall be saved.

MARK 16:16

15.

Neither is there salvation in any other: for there is none other name under heaven given among men, whereby we must be saved.

ACTS 4:12

16.

But we believe that through the grace of the LORD Jesus Christ we shall be saved.

ACTS 15:11

17.

That if thou shalt confess with thy mouth the Lord Jesus, and shall believe in thine heart that God hath raised him from the dead, thou shalt be saved. . . . For whosoever shall call upon the name of the Lord shall be saved.

ROMANS 10:9, 13

18.

With long life will I satisfy him,
and shew him my salvation.

PSALM 91:16

19.

For therefore we both labour and suffer
reproach, because we trust in the living
God, who is the Saviour of all men,
specially of those that believe.

1 TIMOTHY 4:10

20.

Having therefore, brethren, boldness to enter
into the holiest by the blood of Jesus, by a new
and living way, which he hath consecrated for
us. . .let us draw near with a true heart in full
assurance of faith, having our hearts sprinkled
from an evil conscience. . . . Let us hold fast
the profession of our faith without wavering:
(for he is faithful that promised).

HEBREWS 10:19–20, 22–23

ATTITUDE

*David said it best, Lord, when he asked You
to search his heart and know his thoughts.
Please examine me so my heart and thoughts
are right before You. My attitude reflects what
is inside me, and sometimes, maybe more than
I realize, I need an attitude check. I judge
others, and they can sense it. At times I may
think I deserve better, and it makes others feel
as if they are less than I am. Your Word says
I have the mind of Christ. With Your mind in
me help me show Your immense love for others
through my attitude, my words, and my
actions. In Your name, amen.*

21.
Search me, O God, and know my heart:
try me, and know my thoughts: and
see if there be any wicked way in me,
and lead me in the way everlasting.

PSALM 139:23–24

22.

For as he thinketh in his heart, so is he.

PROVERBS 23:7

23.

I know, and am persuaded by the Lord Jesus, that there is nothing unclean of itself: but to him that esteemeth any thing to be unclean, to him it is unclean.

ROMANS 14:14

24.

Now the God of patience and consolation grant you to be like-minded one toward another according to Christ Jesus; that ye may with one mind and one mouth glorify God, even the Father of our Lord Jesus Christ.

ROMANS 15:5–6

25.

Forasmuch then as Christ hath suffered
for us in the flesh, arm yourselves likewise
with the same mind: for he that hath
suffered in the flesh hath ceased from sin.

1 PETER 4:1

26.

Fulfill ye my joy, that ye be likeminded,
having the same love, being of one
accord, of one mind.

PHILIPPIANS 2:2

27.

Let this mind be in you,
which was also in Christ Jesus.

PHILIPPIANS 2:5

28.

Let us therefore, as many as be perfect, be thus
minded: and if in any thing ye be otherwise
minded, God shall reveal even this unto you.

PHILIPPIANS 3:15

29.

Unto the pure all things are pure:
but unto them that are defiled and
unbelieving is nothing pure: but even
their mind and conscience is defiled.

TITUS 1:15

30.

Be renewed in the spirit of your mind.

EPHESIANS 4:23

BELIEF

*Father, do You know how hard it is to believe
You sometimes? It shouldn't be. Look at all
those people who have believed in You since the
beginning of time. How did they do it? Maybe
they wrestled with believing You. Maybe they
doubted. They may not have had as much to go
on as we do today. In the early days they had
word of mouth and experience. But, the fact is,
they believed You. They believed Your promises.
You never failed them. And You have promised
never to fail me. Help me believe in You as
Abraham, Daniel, and Mary did. Thank You,
Father.*

31.

And the people believed: and when they heard
that the LORD had visited the children of Israel,
and that he had looked upon their affliction,
then they bowed their heads and worshipped.

EXODUS 4:31

32.

And he believed in the Lord; and he counted it to him for righteousness.

Genesis 15:6

33.

And Jesus said unto the centurion, Go thy way; and as thou hast believed, so be it done unto thee. And his servant was healed in the selfsame hour.

Matthew 8:13

34.

Then believed they his words; they sang his praise.

Psalm 106:12

35.

Teach me good judgment and knowledge:
for I have believed thy commandments.

PSALM 119:66

36.

Then was the king exceedingly glad for him,
and commanded that they should take Daniel
up out of the den. So Daniel was taken up out
of the den, and no manner of hurt was found
upon him, because he believed in his God.

DANIEL 6:23

37.

I had fainted, unless I had believed
to see the goodness of the LORD
in the land of the living.

PSALM 27:13

38.

As soon as Jesus heard the word that was spoken, he saith unto the ruler of the synagogue, Be not afraid, only believe.

MARK 5:36

39.

Jesus said unto him, If thou canst believe, all things are possible to him that believeth. And straightway the father of the child cried out, and said with tears, Lord, I believe; help thou mine unbelief.

MARK 9:23–24

40.

And blessed is she that believed: for there shall be a performance of those things which were told her from the Lord.

LUKE 1:45

BLESSINGS

Lord, You are the one who deserves the best blessings. You extend blessings to us, and only because of You are we worthy to receive them. Help us seek You first and not what You can give us. Having a wonderful family, a secure job, and a comfortable life may show we are blessed. But what of those who are separated from family, struggling to pay the rent, or living in a homeless shelter? Are they not blessed as well, perhaps in other ways? Simply knowing You and having Your love is the greatest blessing of all. Help us share You with others. In Your name, amen.

41.

And I will make them and the places round about my hill a blessing; and I will cause the shower to come down in his season; there shall be showers of blessing.

EZEKIEL 34:26

42.

The LORD shall command the blessing
upon thee in thy storehouses, and in
all that thou settest thine hand unto;
and he shall bless thee in the land
which the LORD thy God giveth thee.

DEUTERONOMY 28:8

43.

For thou preventest him with the
blessings of goodness: thou settest
a crown of pure gold on his head.

PSALM 21:3

44.

He shall receive the blessing
from the LORD, and righteousness
from the God of his salvation.

PSALM 24:5

45.

Saying with a loud voice, Worthy is the
Lamb that was slain to receive power,
and riches, and wisdom, and strength,
and honour, and glory, and blessing.

REVELATION 5:12

46.

The blessing of the LORD, it maketh
rich, and he addeth no sorrow with it.

PROVERBS 10:22

47.

A faithful man shall abound with
blessings: but he that maketh haste
to be rich shall not be innocent.

PROVERBS 28:20

48.

Blessings are upon the head of the just: but
violence covereth the mouth of the wicked.

PROVERBS 10:6

49.

And all these blessings shall come on thee,
and overtake thee, if thou shalt hearken
unto the voice of the LORD thy God.

DEUTERONOMY 28:2

50.

Blessed be the God and Father of our Lord
Jesus Christ, who hath blessed us with all
spiritual blessings in heavenly places in Christ.

EPHESIANS 1:3

COMFORT

God of all comfort, You surround me with friends and family during difficult seasons. You send the words, the hugs, the practical help to keep me going. Even now, Lord, when the pain has dulled to a distant ache, You still comfort me. You give me pleasant dreams of happy times. When I long to talk about my pain, You send others who have shared in similar heart-aches to comfort me. You keep me going through them and through other friends. Thank You, Lord. Please help me give Your comfort to others. In the name of Jesus, amen.

51.
Yea, though I walk through the valley
of the shadow of death, I will fear
no evil: for thou art with me; thy rod
and thy staff they comfort me.

PSALM 23:4

52.

In the multitude of my thoughts within
me thy comforts delight my soul.

PSALM 94:19

———

53.

This is my comfort in my affliction:
for thy word hath quickened me.

PSALM 119:50

———

54.

But the Comforter, which is the Holy
Ghost, whom the Father will send in
my name, he shall teach you all things,
and bring all things to your remembrance,
whatsoever I have said unto you.

JOHN 14:26

55.

I, even I, am he that comforteth you.

ISAIAH 51:12

56.

Blessed are they that mourn:
for they shall be comforted.

MATTHEW 5:4

57.

Blessed be God, even the Father of our Lord
Jesus Christ, the Father of mercies, and the
God of all comfort; who comforteth us in all
our tribulation, that we may be able to comfort
them which are in any trouble, by the comfort
wherewith we ourselves are comforted of God.

2 CORINTHIANS 1:3–4

58.

And he said unto her, Daughter,
be of good comfort: thy faith hath
made thee whole; go in peace.

Luke 8:48

59.

I will not leave you comfortless:
I will come to you.

John 14:18

60.

Comfort ye, comfort ye
my people, saith your God.

Isaiah 40:1

CONTENTMENT

Father, we are so restless in this world, running hither and yon, staring at our devices, scheduling every minute. It's hard for us to settle down, to sit beside a quiet stream, to gaze at the blue sky, the green trees, and listen to the birds chirp. Let us find that quiet stream, listen for Your voice, and be content in following You. The grass is rarely greener on the other side. Sometimes we learn the hard way. Being satisfied where You have us and with what You have given us is a good gift. You alone satisfy us, and You alone are always with us. Thank You, Father.

61.

And Joshua said, Alas, O Lord God, wherefore hast thou at all brought this people over Jordan, to deliver us into the hand of the Amorites, to destroy us? would to God we had been content, and dwelt on the other side Jordan!

JOSHUA 7:7

62.

The fear of the LORD tendeth to life:
and he that hath it shall abide satisfied;
he shall not be visited with evil.

PROVERBS 19:23

63.

As for me, I will behold thy face in
righteousness: I shall be satisfied,
when I awake, with thy likeness.

PSALM 17:15

64.

Blessed is the man whom thou choosest,
and causest to approach unto thee,
that he may dwell in thy courts: we
shall be satisfied with the goodness
of thy house, even of thy holy temple.

PSALM 65:4

65.

And when Moses heard that,
he was content.

LEVITICUS 10:20

66.

And ye shall eat in plenty, and be satisfied,
and praise the name of the LORD your God,
that hath dealt wondrously with you:
and my people shall never be ashamed.

JOEL 2:26

67.

Not that I speak in respect of want:
for I have learned, in whatsoever state
I am, therewith to be content.

PHILIPPIANS 4:11

68.
But godliness with
contentment is great gain.

1 Timothy 6:6

69.
And having food and raiment
let us be therewith content.

1 Timothy 6:8

70.
Let your conversation be without
covetousness; and be content with
such things as ye have: for he hath said,
I will never leave thee, nor forsake thee.

Hebrews 13:5

COUNSEL

*Wise counsel is Yours, Lord, but how do I tap
into that when I need it? Sometimes I lose my
way, am overwhelmed with the issues facing me
each day. Instead of seeking Your thoughts on a
matter first though, I often turn to others. What
do they know that You don't? Nothing. What
do You know that they don't? Everything. Help
me listen to Your still, small voice within and
be able to discern what is Your voice through
others. Help me know whether the way I take
is the way You have planned for me. Thank You
for being with me, my Wonderful Counselor, no
matter what. Amen.*

71.

Hearken now unto my voice, I will give
thee counsel, and God shall be with thee:
Be thou for the people to God-ward, that
thou mayest bring the causes unto God.

Exodus 18:19

72.

And they said unto him, Ask counsel, we pray
thee, of God, that we may know whether our
way which we go shall be prosperous.

JUDGES 18:5

73.

O Lord, thou art my God; I will exalt
thee, I will praise thy name; for thou
hast done wonderful things; thy counsels
of old are faithfulness and truth.

ISAIAH 25:1

74.

With him is wisdom and strength,
he hath counsel and understanding.

JOB 12:13

75.

Blessed is the man that walketh
not in the counsel of the ungodly,
nor standeth in the way of sinners,
nor sitteth in the seat of the scornful.

PSALM 1:1

76.

I will bless the LORD, who hath
given me counsel: my reins also
instruct me in the night seasons.

PSALM 16:7

77.

A wise man will hear, and will increase
learning: and a man of understanding
shall attain unto wise counsels.

PROVERBS 1:5

78.

We took sweet counsel together, and walked
unto the house of God in company.

PSALM 55:14

79.

And the children of Israel arose, and went up
to the house of God, and asked counsel of
God, and said, Which of us shall go up first
to the battle against the children of Benjamin?
And the LORD said, Judah shall go up first. . . .
(And the children of Israel went up and wept
before the LORD until even, and asked counsel
of the LORD, saying, Shall I go up again to battle
against the children of Benjamin my brother?
And the LORD said, Go up against him.)

JUDGES 20:18, 23

80.

The counsel of the LORD standeth for ever,
the thoughts of his heart to all generations.

PSALM 33:11

DISCIPLINE

*Discipline is not one of my favorite topics,
Father, as You well know. But it's necessary for
life. Your discipline is not hard, though it may
seem so at the time. You have a purpose in it,
and it's for my good. If accepting Your discipline
means my faith will grow stronger, then help
me welcome it. Help me obey Your voice, trust
in You and draw near to You. And help me
remember the lessons learned. When I chafe
under Your correction, please open my eyes to
see Your hand holding mine—as You walk
beside me. Thank You, Father.*

81.

All scripture is given by inspiration of God,
and is profitable for doctrine, for reproof,
for correction, for instruction in righteousness:
that the man of God may be perfect,
thoroughly furnished unto all good works.

2 TIMOTHY 3:16–17

82.

My son, despise not the chastening of the
LORD; neither be weary of his correction.

PROVERBS 3:11

83.

Art thou not from everlasting, O LORD my
God, mine Holy One? we shall not die.
O LORD, thou hast ordained them for
judgment; and, O mighty God, thou
hast established them for correction.

HABAKKUK 1:12

84.

Chasten thy son while there is hope,
and let not thy soul spare for his crying.

PROVERBS 19:18

85.

Train up a child in the way he should go: and when he is old, he will not depart from it.

PROVERBS 22:6

———

86.

Now no chastening for the present seemeth to be joyous, but grievous: nevertheless afterward it yieldeth the peaceable fruit of righteousness unto them which are exercised thereby.

HEBREWS 12:11

———

87.

She obeyed not the voice; she received not correction; she trusted not in the LORD; she drew not near to her God.

ZEPHANIAH 3:2

88.

But the fruit of the Spirit is love, joy,
peace, longsuffering, gentleness,
goodness, faith, meekness, temperance:
against such there is no law.

GALATIANS 5:22–23

89.

For God hath not given us the spirit
of fear; but of power, and of love,
and of a sound mind.

2 TIMOTHY 1:7

90.

Where there is no vision, the people perish:
but he that keepeth the law, happy is he.

PROVERBS 29:18

DUTY

Is it true that my whole duty is to fear—
respect—You, Lord, and keep Your
commandments? That seems so simple.
But how can that make a difference in my
faith? Perhaps in reaping the rewards of
respect and obedience my faith will
strengthen. Respecting You may be easy,
Lord, once I know how to do it, but obeying,
not so easy. If it were easy, I wouldn't need
You. But Your Word reveals the plan: do justly,
love mercy, and walk humbly with You. And
underneath all that: love one another. Please
teach me to follow what is good. In Your
dear name, amen.

91.

And he said to them all, If any man will come
after me, let him deny himself, and take up his
cross daily, and follow me. For whosoever will
save his life shall lose it: but whosoever will
lose his life for my sake, the same shall save it.

Luke 9:23–24

92.

I beseech you therefore, brethren, by the mercies of God, that ye present your bodies a living sacrifice, holy, acceptable unto God, which is your reasonable service. And be not conformed to this world: but be ye transformed by the renewing of your mind, that ye may prove what is that good, and acceptable, and perfect, will of God.

ROMANS 12:1–2

93.

From the rising of the sun unto the going down of the same the LORD's name is to be praised.

PSALM 113:3

94.

Let us hear the conclusion of the whole matter: Fear God, and keep his commandments: for this is the whole duty of man.

ECCLESIASTES 12:13

95.

He hath shewed thee, O man, what is good;
and what doth the Lord require of thee,
but to do justly, and to love mercy, and
to walk humbly with thy God?

MICAH 6:8

96.

Whatsoever thy hand findeth to do, do it
with thy might; for there is no work,
nor device, nor knowledge, nor wisdom,
in the grave, whither thou goest.

ECCLESIASTES 9:10

97.

So likewise ye, when ye shall have done
all those things which are commanded you,
say, We are unprofitable servants: we have
done that which was our duty to do.

LUKE 17:10

98.

Owe no man any thing, but to love
one another: for he that loveth
another hath fulfilled the law.

ROMANS 13:8

99.

Masters, give unto your servants that
which is just and equal; knowing that
ye also have a Master in heaven.

COLOSSIANS 4:1

100.

See that none render evil for evil unto any
man; but ever follow that which is good,
both among yourselves, and to all men.

1 THESSALONIANS 5:15

ENCOURAGEMENT

*The promise You are with me, Lord, gives me
courage to take steps of faith. That's what Your
Word says. But sometimes I forget, and You send
an encouraging word through a friend, a family
member, a song running through my mind. The
best songs are often the psalms. In fact, isn't that
how David encouraged himself—by writing
and singing to You? Help me encourage others
who may need strength for a special task. To
give a cheerful, caring word when they are sad.
To inspire them to write their own psalms. To
remind them You are with them. Let my heart
take courage because You are with me. In Your
dear name, amen.*

101.

Take heed, brethren, lest there be in any of you
an evil heart of unbelief, in departing from the
living God. But exhort one another daily, while
it is called To day; lest any of you be hardened
through the deceitfulness of sin.

HEBREWS 3:12–13

102.

Fear thou not; for I am with thee;
be not dismayed; for I am thy God: I will
strengthen thee; yea, I will help thee: yea,
I will uphold thee with the right hand of
my righteousness. . . . For I the LORD thy
God will hold thy right hand, saying unto
thee, Fear not: I will help thee.

ISAIAH 41:10, 13

103.

Be ye strong therefore, and let not your hands
be weak: for your work shall be rewarded.

2 CHRONICLES 15:7

104.

Say to them that are of a fearful heart,
Be strong, fear not: behold, your God will
come with vengeance, even God with a
recompence; he will come and save you.

ISAIAH 35:4

105.

Be strong, all ye people of the land,
saith the LORD, and work: for I am
with you, saith the LORD of hosts.

HAGGAI 2:4

106.

And the night following the Lord stood by
him, and said, Be of good cheer, Paul: for
as thou hast testified of me in Jerusalem,
so must thou bear witness also at Rome.

ACTS 23:11

107.

And let us consider one another to provoke
unto love and to good works: not forsaking the
assembling of ourselves together, as the manner
of some is: but exhorting one another: and so
much the more, as ye see the day approaching.

HEBREWS 10:24–25

108.

Watch ye, stand fast in the faith,
quit you like men, be strong.

1 Corinthians 16:13

109.

Finally, my brethren, be strong in the
Lord, and in the power of his might.

Ephesians 6:10

110.

Thou therefore, my son, be strong in
the grace that is in Christ Jesus.

2 Timothy 2:1

ENEMIES

*Love my enemies, Lord? Is that even possible?
How can I when they come against me every
time they see me? Am I to turn the other cheek?
Let them walk over me? Will praying for my
enemies work? I haven't seen a change in them,
Lord. I see only their hatred. And it hurts.
Especially when it is my own flesh and blood.
Despitefully use me? Curse me? Oh yes. Please
help my heart, Lord, to be Your heart. Please
help me love when nothing but hatred is evident.
Please help me leave them in Your hands. You
desire healing. For Your sake, amen.*

111.
For we wrestle not against flesh and blood,
but against principalities, against powers,
against the rulers of the darkness of this world,
against spiritual wickedness in high places.
Wherefore take unto you the whole armour of
God, that ye may be able to withstand in the
evil day, and having done all, to stand.

Ephesians 6:12–13

112.

Thy right hand, O Lord, is become
glorious in power: thy right hand,
O Lord, hath dashed in pieces the enemy.

Exodus 15:6

113.

So let all thine enemies perish, O Lord:
but let them that love him be as the sun
when he goeth forth in his might. And
the land had rest forty years.

Judges 5:31

114.

He delivereth me from mine enemies: yea,
thou liftest me up above those that rise up
against me: thou hast delivered me from the
violent man. Therefore will I give thanks
unto thee, O Lord, among the heathen,
and sing praises unto thy name.

Psalm 18:48–49

115.

Let God arise, let his enemies be scattered:
let them also that hate him flee before him.

PSALM 68:1

116.

Let this be the reward of mine adversaries
from the LORD, and of them that speak evil
against my soul. But do thou for me, O GOD
the Lord, for thy name's sake: because thy
mercy is good, deliver thou me.

PSALM 109:20–21

117.

If thine enemy be hungry, give him bread to
eat: and if he be thirsty, give him water to
drink: for thou shalt heap coals of fire upon
his head, and the LORD shall reward thee.

PROVERBS 25:21–22

118.

Rejoice not when thine enemy falleth, and let not thine heart be glad when he stumbleth.

PROVERBS 24:17

119.

But I say unto you, Love your enemies, bless them that curse you, do good to them that hate you, and pray for them which despitefully use you, and persecute you.

MATTHEW 5:44

120.

And they stoned Stephen, calling upon God, and saying, Lord Jesus, receive my spirit. And he kneeled down, and cried with a loud voice, Lord, lay not this sin to their charge. And when he had said this, he fell asleep.

ACTS 7:59–60

FAITH

How is it, Lord, that some people find it easy to have faith in You, while others find it nearly impossible? Is it because some have a simpler nature and are more willing to believe? Is it more educated folks who get stuck and can't believe in the supernatural? Would I believe in You if I'd been born in another country, where those who believe in You are persecuted, even murdered? My prayer is that You will increase my faith. And please give the gift of faith to my loved ones and friends—to everyone in the world. Our faith makes You happy. In Your name, amen.

121.

Let us draw near with a true heart in full assurance of faith, having our hearts sprinkled from an evil conscience, and our bodies washed with pure water. Let us hold fast the profession of our faith without wavering: (for he is faithful that promised).

HEBREWS 10:22–23

122.

Fight the good fight of faith, lay hold on eternal life, whereunto thou art also called, and hast professed a good profession before many witnesses.

1 TIMOTHY 6:12

123.

Therefore we conclude that a man is justified by faith without the deeds of the law.

ROMANS 3:28

124.

Therefore being justified by faith, we have peace with God through our Lord Jesus Christ: by whom also we have access by faith into this grace wherein we stand, and rejoice in hope of the glory of God.

ROMANS 5:1–2

125.

So then faith cometh by hearing,
and hearing by the word of God.

ROMANS 10:17

126.

But without faith it is impossible to please
him: for he that cometh to God must
believe that he is, and that he is a rewarder
of them that diligently seek him.

HEBREWS 11:6

127.

Now the end of the commandment is
charity out of a pure heart, and of a good
conscience, and of faith unfeigned.

1 TIMOTHY 1:5

128.

For we walk by faith,
not by sight.

2 CORINTHIANS 5:7

129.

And the apostles said unto
the Lord, Increase our faith.

LUKE 17:5

130.

Now faith is the substance of things hoped
for, the evidence of things not seen.

HEBREWS 11:1

FEAR

How many times, Father, have You told me not to fear? So many I should have learned it by now. Perhaps You told me not to fear so often because You knew I would and knew I had no reason to. After all, You are with me every moment of every day—and night. It is at night that fear creeps in, keeping me awake, my heart pounding in my ears. But day and night are the same to You, and You bring only peace. Help me to have Your peace that drives out all my fears, both day and night. In the powerful name of Jesus, amen.

131.

And the LORD appeared unto him [Isaac] the same night, and said, I am the God of Abraham thy father: fear not, for I am with thee, and will bless thee, and multiply thy seed for my servant Abraham's sake.

GENESIS 26:24

132.

And the LORD said unto him, Peace be
unto thee; fear not: thou shalt not die.

JUDGES 6:23

133.

But now thus saith the LORD that created thee,
O Jacob, and he that formed thee, O Israel,
Fear not: for I have redeemed thee. I have
called thee by thy name; thou art mine. When
thou passest through the waters, I will be with
thee; and through the rivers, they shall not
overflow thee: when thou walkest through the
fire, thou shalt not be burned; neither shall the
flame kindle upon thee. For I am the LORD thy
God, the Holy One of Israel, thy Saviour.

ISAIAH 43:1–3

134.

And he answered, Fear not: for they that be
with us are more than they that be with them.

2 KINGS 6:16

135.

And a certain woman, which had an issue of
blood twelve years. . .touched his garment. . . .
And straightway the fountain of her blood was
dried up. . . . And he looked round about to
see her that had done this thing. But the woman
fearing and trembling, knowing what was done
in her, came and fell down before him, and
told him all the truth. And he said unto her,
Daughter, thy faith hath made thee whole:
go in peace, and be whole of thy plague.

MARK 5:25, 27, 29, 32–34

136.

Fear thou not; for I am with thee: be not
dismayed; for I am thy God: I will strengthen
thee: yea, I will help thee: yea, I will uphold
thee with the right hand of my righteousness.

ISAIAH 41:10

137.

The fear of man bringeth a snare: but whoso
putteth his trust in the LORD shall be safe.

PROVERBS 29:25

138.

Are not two sparrows sold for a farthing?
And one of them shall not fall on the ground
without your Father. But the very hairs of your
head are all numbered. Fear ye not therefore,
ye are of more value than many sparrows.

Matthew 10:29–31

139.

And the angel said unto her, Fear not, Mary:
for thou hast found favor with God. And,
behold, thou shalt conceive in thy womb, and
bring forth a son, and shalt call his name Jesus.
He shall be great, and shall be called the Son of
the Highest: and the Lord God shall give unto
him the throne of his father David: and he shall
reign over the house of Jacob for ever; and of
his kingdom there shall be no end.

Luke 1:30–33

140.

And, lo, the angel of the Lord came upon
them, and the glory of the Lord shone round
about them, and they were sore afraid. And
the angel said unto them, Fear not: for,
behold, I bring you good tidings of great
joy, which shall be to all people.

Luke 2:9–10

FORGIVENESS

*Thank You, Lord, for giving Your life for me
on the cross. Thank You for Your sacrifice that
covers all my sins, past, present, and future.
Unlike the sacrifices of old, Your blood washes
away my sins and makes me clean and pure in
Your sight. I have no guilt. I don't need to beg.
You have done it all. How can I not extend that
same forgiveness to others when they wrong me?
How can I not offer a clean slate to someone else
who offends me? In that way I show them Your
forgiveness. It might be hard because I am only
human. But You are God, and You have forgiven
so much more. Thank You, Lord.*

141.
Take heed to yourselves: If thy brother
trespass against thee, rebuke him: and if
he repent, forgive him. And if he trespass
against thee seven times in a day, and seven
times in a day turn again to thee, saying,
I repent: thou shalt forgive him.

Luke 17:3–4

142.

But they and our fathers dealt proudly and hardened their necks, and hearkened not to thy commandments, and refused to obey, neither were mindful of thy wonders that thou didst among them; but hardened their necks, and in their rebellion appointed a captain to return to their bondage; but thou art a God ready to pardon, gracious and merciful, slow to anger, and of great kindness, and forsookest them not.

NEHEMIAH 9:16–17

143.

Bless the LORD, O my soul, and forget not all his benefits: who forgiveth all thine iniquities: who healeth all thy diseases.

PSALM 103:2–3

144.

If thou, LORD, shouldest mark iniquities, O Lord, who shall stand? But there is forgiveness with thee, that thou mayest be feared.

PSALM 130:3–4

145.

In whom we have redemption through
his blood, the forgiveness of sins,
according to the riches of his grace.

EPHESIANS 1:7

146.

And be ye kind one to another, tenderhearted,
forgiving one another, even as God for
Christ's sake hath forgiven you.

EPHESIANS 4:32

147.

And every priest standeth daily ministering
and offering oftentimes the same sacrifices,
which can never take away sins: but this man,
after he had offered one sacrifice for sins for
ever, sat down on the right hand of God. . . .
This is the covenant that I will make with
them after those days, saith the Lord, I will put
my laws into their hearts, and in their minds
will I write them; and their sins and iniquities
will I remember no more.

HEBREWS 10:11–12, 16–17

148.

And when ye stand praying, forgive, if ye have
ought against any: that your Father also which
is in heaven may forgive you your trespasses.
But if ye do not forgive, neither will your Father
which is in heaven forgive your trespasses.

MARK 11:25–26

149.

And the prayer of faith shall save the sick,
and the Lord shall raise him up; and if he have
committed sins, they shall be forgiven him.

JAMES 5:15

150.

If we confess our sins, he is faithful
and just to forgive us our sins, and to
cleanse us from all unrighteousness.

1 JOHN 1:9

GENEROSITY

Father, have I been as generous with You and with others as You have been with me? I hold on to my possessions, my money, my heart. You give over and above. Do You withhold good because someone doesn't walk with You? Your Word says Your sun rises on the evil and the good and You send rain on the just and the unjust. Does that mean I am to be as generous and giving with someone who doesn't agree with me, whether spiritually, politically, or socially? Do You distinguish between the poor and the rich? No, You give freely, more than enough, and call me to do the same. Please open my heart to You and to others. Amen.

151.

Give, and it shall be given unto you; good measure, pressed down, and shaken together, and running over, shall men give into your bosom. For with the same measure that ye mete withal it shall be measured to you again.

Luke 6:38

152.

And they spake unto Moses, saying,
The people bring much more than enough
for the service of the work, which the
LORD commanded to make.

EXODUS 36:5

153.

Moreover, because I have set my affection to
the house of my God, I have of mine own
proper good, of gold and silver, which I have
given to the house of my God, over and above
all that I have prepared for the holy house.

1 CHRONICLES 29:3

154.

And he looked up, and saw the rich men
casting their gifts into the treasury. And he saw
also a certain poor widow casting in thither two
mites. And he said, Of a truth I say unto you,
that this poor widow hath cast in more than
they all: for all these have of their abundance
cast in unto the offerings of God: but she of her
penury hath cast in all the living that she had.

LUKE 21:1–4

155.

And Zacchaeus stood, and said unto the Lord: Behold, Lord, the half of my goods I give to the poor; and if I have taken any thing from any man by false accusation, I restore him fourfold.

LUKE 19:8

156.

Moreover, brethren, we do you to wit of the grace of God bestowed on the churches of Macedonia: how that in a great trial of affliction the abundance of their joy and their deep poverty abounded unto the riches of their liberality. . . . Praying us with much entreaty that we would receive the gift, and take upon us the fellowship of the ministering to the saints. And this they did, not as we hoped, but first gave their own selves to the Lord, and unto us by the will of God.

2 CORINTHIANS 8:1–2, 4–5

157.

The liberal soul shall be made fat: and he that watereth shall be watered also himself.

PROVERBS 11:25

158.

He that hath a bountiful eye shall be blessed;
for he giveth of his bread to the poor.

PROVERBS 22:9

159.

Blessed is he that considereth the poor:
the LORD will deliver him in time of trouble.

PSALM 41:1

160.

Neither was there any among them that lacked:
for as many as were possessors of lands or
houses sold them, and brought the prices of
the things that were sold, and laid them down
at the apostles' feet; and distribution was made
unto every man according as he had need.

ACTS 4:34–35

GENTLENESS

*Lord, what did the psalmist mean when he said
Your gentleness had made him great? Can our
gentle approach to others make them great?
Surely our gentle speech can help calm a storm
of anger. Instead of snapping we can respond
with kind words when someone yells at us or
calls us names. A shepherd is gentle with his
flock; he doesn't roughhouse them; he doesn't
abuse them. He leads them gently with love,
carrying them next to his heart. That's how You
are with us. You carry us next to Your heart.
Help us be gentle with those around us, even
the difficult ones. You are the gentle Shepherd.
In Your name, amen.*

161.
He shall feed his flock like a shepherd:
he shall gather the lambs with his arm and
carry them in his bosom, and shall gently
lead those that are with young.

ISAIAH 40:11

162.

Thou hast also given me the shield of thy
salvation: and thy right hand hath holden me
up, and thy gentleness hath made me great.

PSALM 18:35

163.

A soft answer turneth away wrath:
but grievous words stir up anger.

PROVERBS 15:1

164.

Now I Paul myself beseech you by
the meekness and gentleness of Christ,
who in presence am base among you,
but being absent am bold toward you.

2 CORINTHIANS 10:1

165.

And the servant of the Lord must
not strive; but be gentle unto all
men, apt to teach, patient.

2 TIMOTHY 2:24

166.

A bruised reed shall he not break and
the smoking flax shall he not quench:
he shall bring forth judgment unto truth.

ISAIAH 42:3

167.

But we were gentle among you, even
as a nurse cherisheth her children.

1 THESSALONIANS 2:7

168.
But the fruit of the Spirit is. . .gentleness.

GALATIANS 5:22

_____

169.
To speak evil of no man, to be no brawlers,
but gentle, shewing all meekness unto all men.

TITUS 3:2

_____

170.
Servants, be subject to your masters
with all fear; not only to the good
and gentle, but also to the froward.

1 PETER 2:18

GOD'S LOVE

*Nothing can separate me from Your love, Father.
Not even life itself. What a promise. And it isn't
a love that lasts a day or a month or a year. It
lasts my whole life, from beginning to end. Even
after my life on earth is through, You will love
me still in heaven with You. How can my mind
comprehend this? It isn't through anything I
have done; rather it is what You have revealed
in my heart. You came to me in my brokenness.
You answered the cry of my heart for love. Yours
is the only love that satisfies, that drives out
fear, that changes lives. You are Love.*

171.

But God, who is rich in mercy, for his great
love wherewith he loved us, even when we
were dead in sins, hath quickened us together
with Christ, (by grace ye are saved;) and hath
raised us up together, and made us sit together
in heavenly places in Christ Jesus.

Ephesians 2:4–6

172.

The LORD hath appeared of old unto
me, saying, Yea, I have loved thee
with an everlasting love: therefore with
lovingkindness have I drawn thee.

JEREMIAH 31:3

173.

For God so loved the world, that
he gave his only begotten Son, that
whosoever believeth in him should
not perish, but have everlasting life.

JOHN 3:16

174.

In this was manifested the love of God toward
us, because that God sent his only begotten
Son into the world, that we might live through
him. Herein is love, not that we loved God,
but that he loved us, and sent his Son to
be the propitiation for our sins.

1 JOHN 4:9–10

175.

For the Father himself loveth you,
because ye have loved me, and have
believed that I came out from God.

John 16:27

176.

And hope maketh not ashamed; because the
love of God is shed abroad in our hearts by
the Holy Ghost which is given unto us.

Romans 5:5

177.

For I am persuaded, that neither death, nor
life, nor angels, nor principalities, nor powers,
nor things present, nor things to come, nor
height, nor depth, nor any other creature, shall
be able to separate us from the love of God,
which is in Christ Jesus our Lord.

Romans 8:38–39

178.

But God commendeth his love
toward us, in that, while we were
yet sinners, Christ died for us.

ROMANS 5:8

179.

Behold, what manner of love the Father
hath bestowed upon us, that we should be
called the sons of God: therefore the world
knoweth us not, because it knew him not.

1 JOHN 3:1

180.

And we have known and believed
the love that God hath to us. God is
love; and he that dwelleth in love
dwelleth in God, and God in him.

1 JOHN 4:16

GOD'S PROVISION

Father, I remember Your promise to supply all my needs. What if my need is for water or food or shelter or even love? What if I am home-less? How will You supply all my needs? Do the homeless seek You for shelter—and not find it? What of the fires and storms of life that destroy our homes, our loved ones? How then can we believe You provide? You have provided for us in the past. Help us remember those times and trust You for the future. And help us find rest in Your secret place, under Your wings of protection. In the name of Jesus, amen.

181.

For the LORD thy God hath blessed thee in all the works of thy hand: he knoweth thy walking through this great wilderness: these forty years the LORD thy God hath been with thee: thou hast lacked nothing.

DEUTERONOMY 2:7

182.

And the ravens brought him bread and flesh in the morning, and bread and flesh in the evening; and he drank of the brook.

1 Kings 17:6

183.

For he maketh his sun to rise on the evil and on the good, and sendeth rain on the just and on the unjust.

Matthew 5:45

184.

He that dwelleth in the secret place of the most High shall abide under the shadow of the Almighty. I will say of the Lord, He is my refuge and my fortress: my God; in him will I trust. . . . He shall cover thee with his feathers, and under his wings shalt thou trust: his truth shall be thy shield and buckler.

Psalm 91:1–2, 4

185.

I will lift up mine eyes unto the hills, from whence cometh my help. My help cometh from the LORD, which made heaven and earth. He will not suffer thy foot to be moved; he that keepeth thee will not slumber. . . . The LORD is thy keeper: the LORD is thy shade upon thy right hand. . . . The LORD shall preserve thee from all evil: he shall preserve thy soul.

PSALM 121:1–3, 5, 7

186.

As the apple tree among the trees of the wood, so is my beloved among the sons. I sat down under his shadow with great delight, and his fruit was sweet to my taste. He brought me to the banqueting house, and his banner over me was love.

SONG OF SOLOMON 2:3–4

187.

But my God shall supply all your need according to his riches in glory by Christ Jesus.

PHILIPPIANS 4:19

188.

Because thou hast been my help, therefore
in the shadow of thy wings will I rejoice.

PSALM 63:7

189.

Behold the fowls of the air: for they sow not,
neither do they reap, nor gather into barns;
yet your heavenly Father feedeth them.
Are ye not much better than they?

MATTHEW 6:26

190.

And he commanded the multitude to
sit down on the grass, and took the five
loaves, and the two fishes, and looking up
to heaven, he blessed, and brake, and gave
the loaves to his disciples, and the disciples
to the multitude. And they did all eat, and
were filled: and they took up of the fragments
that remained twelve baskets full. And they
that had eaten were about five thousand
men, beside women and children.

MATTHEW 14:19–21

GOD'S WILL

What is Your will, Lord? How can I discover it? And once I know it, will I want to do it? The psalmist said he delighted to do Your will. But what if I don't? What if I think my will is better? It seems though, that the psalmist, the early believers, the Gospel writers, concluded that the will of the Father was not just better than their own, but best. Perfect. Please renew my mind that I too may discover what is Your perfect will in everything. And let me say with my whole heart, the will of the Lord be done. Amen.

191.
Servants, be obedient to them that are your masters according to the flesh, with fear and trembling, in singleness of your heart, as unto Christ; not with eyeservice, as menpleasers; but as the servants of Christ, doing the will of God from the heart.

EPHESIANS 6:5–6

192.

I delight to do thy will, O my God:
yea, thy law is within my heart.

PSALM 40:8

193.

Teach me to do thy will: for thou
art my God: thy spirit is good;
lead me into the land of uprightness.

PSALM 143:10

194.

He went away again the second time,
and prayed, saying, O my Father,
if this cup may not pass away from me,
except I drink it, thy will be done.

MATTHEW 26:42

195.

For whosoever shall do the will of my Father which is in heaven, the same is my brother, and sister, and mother.

MATTHEW 12:50

196.

Thy kingdom come. Thy will be done in earth, as it is in heaven.

MATTHEW 6:10

197.

I can of mine own self do nothing: as I hear, I judge: and my judgment is just: because I seek not mine own will, but the will of the Father which hath sent me.

JOHN 5:30

198.

And when he would not be persuaded, we
ceased, saying, The will of the Lord be done.

Acts 21:14

199.

And be not conformed to this world: but be
ye transformed by the renewing of your mind,
that ye may prove what is that good, and
acceptable, and perfect, will of God.

Romans 12:2

200.

And the world passeth away, and the
lust thereof: but he that doeth the
will of God abideth for ever.

1 John 2:17

GRACE

Your grace is amazing, Lord. But what is grace, really? And what makes it so amazing? It is Your gift to us, Your unmerited favor. Freely given, not earned. You have saved us by Your grace. You have grown grace within us. You strengthen our faith with grace. When we are weak, You tell us Your grace is enough. We have done nothing to deserve it. That, in fact, is what makes it grace. It is ours, but only because of what You have done on the cross. Help us extend that grace to others who need You as much as we do. Thank You, Lord.

201.

O my God, incline thine ear, and hear; open thine eyes, and behold our desolations, and the city which is called by thy name: for we do not present our supplications before thee for our righteousness, but for thy great mercies.

DANIEL 9:18

202.

I am crucified with Christ: nevertheless I live;
yet not I, but Christ liveth in me: and the life
which I now live in the flesh I live by the faith
of the Son of God, who loved me, and gave
himself for me. I do not frustrate the grace of
God: for if righteousness come by the law,
then Christ is dead in vain.

GALATIANS 2:20–21

203.

And the child grew, and waxed strong
in spirit, filled with wisdom: and the
grace of God was upon him.

LUKE 2:40

204.

But by the grace of God I am what I am:
and his grace which was bestowed upon
me was not in vain; but I laboured more
abundantly than they all: yet not I, but
the grace of God which was with me.

1 CORINTHIANS 15:10

205.

And he said unto me, My grace is sufficient
for thee: for my strength is made perfect
in weakness. Most gladly therefore will I
rather glory in my infirmities, that the
power of Christ may rest upon me.

2 CORINTHIANS 12:9

206.

For the LORD God is a sun and shield: the LORD
will give grace and glory: no good thing will
he withhold from them that walk uprightly.

PSALM 84:11

207.

For by grace are ye saved through faith;
and that not of yourselves: it is the gift of
God: not of works, lest any man should boast.

EPHESIANS 2:8–9

208.
But unto every one of us is given
grace according to the measure
of the gift of Christ.

EPHESIANS 4:7

209.
But he giveth more grace. Wherefore
he saith, God resisteth the proud,
but giveth grace unto the humble.

JAMES 4:6

210.
The grace of our Lord Jesus
Christ be with you all. Amen.

REVELATION 22:21

GRATITUDE

We have so much to be thankful for, Lord. You have seen to that. Even if You never did another thing for us, we could still give You thanks for the rest of our lives. Your mercy lasts forever. You never leave us. You give us direction. You hold us in Your everlasting arms. You give us present and eternal life. Thank You, Lord! Thank You so much for Your goodness to us. When we do not see it, let us give You our thanks anyway. When we do not feel it, let us whisper our thanks to You. Let our hearts be always grateful to You simply because You are You. In Your dear name, amen.

211.

I thank thee, and praise thee, O thou God of my fathers, who hast given me wisdom and might, and hast made known unto me now what we desired of thee: for thou hast now made known unto us the king's matter.

Daniel 2:23

212.

When thou hast eaten and art full, then thou shalt bless the LORD thy God for the good land which he hath given thee.

DEUTERONOMY 8:10

213.

Enter into his gates with thanksgiving, and into his courts with praise: be thankful unto him and bless his name.

PSALM 100:4

214.

O give thanks unto the LORD, for he is good: for his mercy endureth for ever. . . . And let them sacrifice the sacrifices of thanksgiving, and declare his works with rejoicing.

PSALM 107:1, 22

215.

At midnight I will rise to give thanks unto
thee because of thy righteous judgments.

PSALM 119:62

216.

As ye have therefore received Christ Jesus
the Lord, so walk ye in him: rooted
and built up in him, and stablished in
the faith, as ye have been taught,
abounding therein with thanksgiving.

COLOSSIANS 2:6–7

217.

But thanks be to God, which giveth us the
victory through our Lord Jesus Christ.

1 CORINTHIANS 15:57

218.

Thanks be unto God for
his unspeakable gift.

2 CORINTHIANS 9:15

219.

In every thing give thanks: for this is the
will of God in Christ Jesus concerning you.

1 THESSALONIANS 5:18

220.

And I thank Christ Jesus our Lord, who hath
enabled me, for that he counted me faithful,
putting me into the ministry.

1 TIMOTHY 1:12

GUIDANCE

Father, I cling to the promise that You will instruct me and teach me in the way I should go, keeping watch over me. In fact, many times throughout my life You have reminded me of that promise. I need Your guidance. I am tempted to go my own way and too often do. Then I must ask You to fix the mess I have created. A decision may seem right at the time, but it turns out not to be. Then I remember I didn't ask You to lead me. But out of Your immense love You still point me in the right direction. In the midst of turmoil, lead me beside the still waters. In the name of Jesus, amen.

221.

And I will bring the blind by a way that they knew not; I will lead them in paths that they have not known: I will make darkness light before them, and crooked things straight. These things will I do unto them, and not forsake them.

Isaiah 42:16

222.

Lead me, O Lord, in thy righteousness
because of mine enemies; make thy
way straight before my face.

PSALM 5:8

223.

The Lord is my shepherd: I shall not want.
He maketh me to lie down in green pastures:
he leadeth me beside the still waters.

PSALM 23:1–2

224.

Lead me in thy truth, and teach me:
for thou art the God of my salvation:
on thee do I wait all the day.

PSALM 25:5

225.

The meek will he guide in judgment:
and the meek will he teach his way.

PSALM 25:9

226.

I will instruct thee and teach thee
in the way which thou shalt go:
I will guide thee with mine eye.

PSALM 32:8

227.

When he, the Spirit of truth, is come,
he will guide you into all truth: for he
shall not speak of himself: but whatsoever
he shall hear, that shall he speak: and
he will shew you things to come.

JOHN 16:13

228.

For this God is our God for ever and ever:
he will be our guide even unto death.

PSALM 48:14

229.

And thine ears shall hear a word behind
thee, saying, This is the way, walk ye
in it, when ye turn to the right hand,
and when ye turn to the left.

ISAIAH 30:21

230.

And when he putteth forth his own sheep,
he goeth before them, and the sheep
follow him for they know his voice.

JOHN 10:4

HONESTY

*Honesty is the best policy, isn't it, Father? Or so
I was taught. But how often I fail to live up to
that. You delight in honesty. You guide me with
integrity. You teach me to walk in Your ways.
You do not lie. You cannot because You are God.
You speak truth to me. But if someone is not
honest with or about me, how do I refrain from
anger? Help me to think on what is true. Help
me speak the truth in a loving way to myself
and to others. In Jesus' name, amen.*

231.
I exhort therefore, that, first of all,
supplications, prayers, intercessions, and
giving of thanks, be made for all men;
for kings and for all that are in authority; that
we may lead a quiet and peaceable life in all
godliness and honesty. For this is good and
acceptable in the sight of God our Savior; who
will have all men to be saved, and to come
unto the knowledge of the truth.

1 Timothy 2:1–4

232.

Ye shall do no unrighteousness in judgment, in meteyard, in weight, or in measure. Just balances, just weights, a just ephah, and a just hin, shall ye have: I am the LORD your God, which brought you out of the land of Egypt.

LEVITICUS 19:35–36

233.

Moreover they reckoned not with the men, into whose hand they delivered the money to be bestowed on workmen: for they dealt faithfully.

2 KINGS 12:15

234.

Finally, brethren, whatsoever things are true, whatsoever things are honest, whatsoever things are just, whatsoever things are pure, whatsoever things are lovely, whatsoever things are of good report; if there be any virtue, and if there be any praise, think on these things.

PHILIPPIANS 4:8

235.

That we henceforth be no more children, tossed to and fro, and carried about with every wind of doctrine, by the sleight of men, and cunning craftiness, whereby they lie in wait to deceive; but speaking the truth in love, may grow up into him in all things, which is the head, even Christ.

EPHESIANS 4:14–15

236.

The getting of treasures by a lying tongue is a vanity tossed to and fro of them that seek death.

PROVERBS 21:6

237.

As the partridge sitteth on eggs, and hatcheth them not; so he that getteth riches, and not by right, shall leave them in the midst of his days, and at his end shall be a fool.

JEREMIAH 17:11

238.

A false balance is abomination to the
LORD: but a just weight is his delight.

PROVERBS 11:1

———

239.

Providing for honest things, not only in the
sight of the Lord, but also in the sight of men.

2 CORINTHIANS 8:21

———

240.

Wherefore putting away lying, speak
every man truth with his neighbour:
for we are members one of another.

EPHESIANS 4:25

HOPE

Your resurrection from the dead gives me hope, Lord Jesus—hope through Your victory over death. Hope for life here on earth. Hope for my future in heaven. My hope is in You. I have no one else, nothing else of substance in which to put my hope. Yes, I can put my hope in a job, marriage, friends, cars, abilities, money, or even electronic devices. But not one of them will last. You alone are everlasting. My faith and my hope are in You, Lord Jesus. My heart waits for You. You are my anchor, steady and strong. I love You. In Your name, amen.

241.

We give thanks to God and the Father of our Lord Jesus Christ, praying always for you, since we heard of your faith in Christ Jesus, and of the love which ye have to all the saints, for the hope which is laid up for you in heaven, whereof ye heard before in the word of the truth of the gospel.

COLOSSIANS 1:3–5

242.

Be of good courage, and he shall strengthen
your heart, all ye that hope in the LORD.

PSALM 31:24

243.

Wherein God, willing more abundantly
to shew unto the heirs of promise the
immutability of his counsel, confirmed it
by an oath: that by two immutable things,
in which it was impossible for God to lie,
we might have a strong consolation, who
have fled for refuge to lay hold upon the
hope set before us: which hope we have as
an anchor of the soul, both sure and stedfast,
and which entereth into that within the veil.

HEBREWS 6:17–19

244.

And now, Lord, what wait I for?
my hope is in thee.

PSALM 39:7

245.

Why art thou cast down, O my soul? And why
art thou disquieted within me? Hope thou
in God: for I shall yet praise him, who is the
health of my countenance, and my God.

PSALM 42:11

246.

For we are saved by hope: but hope that is seen
is not hope: for what a man seeth, why doth
he yet hope for? But if we hope for that we see
not, then do we with patience wait for it.

ROMANS 8:24–25

247.

Blessed be the God and Father of our
Lord Jesus Christ, which according to his
abundant mercy hath begotten us again
unto a lively hope by the resurrection
of Jesus Christ from the dead.

1 PETER 1:3

248.

And have hope toward God, which
they themselves also allow, that there
shall be a resurrection of the dead,
both of the just and unjust.

Acts 24:15

249.

For thou art my hope, O Lord God:
thou art my trust from my youth.

Psalm 71:5

250.

But sanctify the Lord God in your hearts:
and be ready always to give an answer to
every man that asketh you a reason of the
hope that is in you with meekness and fear.

1 Peter 3:15

HOSPITALITY

*Father, Your Word says that we should not
neglect to show hospitality to others. But do
You see that trait in me? Why do I get nervous
when I invite friends over for dinner? I want
everything to be perfect, but I know perfection is
unattainable. And does that really matter? Do
my guests care? Doesn't it matter more that my
guests feel loved and cared for and comfortable?
Help me remember that and open my heart and
my home. Help me share Your love with others
by welcoming friends and showing hospitality to
strangers. In Your Son's gracious name, amen.*

251.
Let a little water, I pray you, be fetched, and
wash your feet, and rest yourselves under the
tree: and I will fetch a morsel of bread, and
comfort ye your hearts: after that ye shall pass
on: for therefore are ye come to your servant.
And they said, So do, as thou hast said.

GENESIS 18:4–5

252.

And it came to pass, as Jesus sat at meat in the house, behold, many publicans and sinners came and sat down with him and his disciples.

MATTHEW 9:10

253.

And when Jesus came to the place, he looked up, and saw him, and said unto him, Zacchaeus, make haste, and come down; for to day I must abide at thy house. And he made haste, and came down, and received him joyfully. And when they saw it, they all murmured, saying, That he was gone to be guest with a man that is a sinner.

LUKE 19:5–7

254.

Distributing to the necessity of saints; given to hospitality.

ROMANS 12:13

255.

And the third day there was a marriage in
Cana of Galilee: and the mother of Jesus
was there: and both Jesus was called,
and his disciples, to the marriage.

JOHN 2:1–2

256.

And when he had brought them into his
house, he set meat before them, and rejoiced,
believing in God with all his house.

ACTS 16:34

257.

But they constrained him, saying, Abide with
us: for it is toward evening, and the day is far
spent. And he went in to tarry with them.

LUKE 24:29

258.

A bishop then must be blameless, the husband
of one wife, vigilant, sober, of good behaviour,
given to hospitality, apt to teach.

1 Timothy 3:2

259.

For a bishop must be. . .a lover of
hospitality, a lover of good men,
sober, just, holy, temperate.

Titus 1:7–8

260.

Use hospitality one to another
without grudging.

1 Peter 4:9

HUMILITY

Lord, how can I be anything but humble when I am with You? Each day I am on my knees because there I remember You are far greater than I am and I owe my life to You. Every breath I breathe is from You. Every bit of love in my life is from You. Every friend is a gift from You. Every good thing in my life is from You. I have nothing and can do nothing apart from You. You are my strength made perfect in my weakness. Even my faith comes only from You. I believe because You have given me the gift of faith. Thank You, Lord.

261.

For thus saith the high and lofty One that inhabiteth eternity, whose name is Holy; I dwell in the high and holy place, with him also that is of a contrite and humble spirit, to revive the spirit of the humble, and to revive the heart of the contrite ones.

ISAIAH 57:15

262.

Lord, my heart is not haughty, nor mine eyes lofty: neither do I exercise myself in great matters, or in things too high for me.

PSALM 131:1

263.

Jesus knowing that the Father had given all things into his hands, and that he was come from God, and went to God; he riseth from supper, and laid aside his garments; and took a towel, and girded himself. After that he poureth water into a basin, and began to wash the disciples' feet, and to wipe them with the towel wherewith he was girded.

JOHN 13:3–5

264.

Better it is to be of an humble spirit with the lowly, than to divide the spoil with the proud.

PROVERBS 16:19

265.

A man's pride shall bring him low: but
honour shall uphold the humble in spirit.

PROVERBS 29:23

266.

But ye shall not be so: but he that is greatest
among you, let him be as the younger; and he
that is chief, as he that doth serve. For whether
is greater, he that sitteth at meat, or he that
serveth: is not he that sitteth at meat? But I
am among you as he that serveth.

LUKE 22:26–27

267.

For I say, through the grace given unto me, to
every man that is among you, not to think of
himself more highly than he ought to think;
but to think soberly, according as God hath
dealt to every man the measure of faith.

ROMANS 12:3

268.

Humble yourselves in the sight of
the Lord, and he shall lift you up.

JAMES 4:10

269.

Likewise, ye younger, submit yourselves
unto the elder. Yea, all of you be subject one
to another, and be clothed with humility:
for God resisteth the proud, and giveth grace
to the humble. Humble yourselves therefore
under the mighty hand of God, that he
may exalt you in due time.

1 PETER 5:5–6

270.

By humility and the fear of the LORD
are riches, and honour, and life.

PROVERBS 22:4

INTEGRITY

Father, help me to have integrity in all my dealings with others—in my work and in my leisure, with family, friends, and strangers. Help me be faithful in what You have set before me, whether it is pleasant or unpleasant. To walk with integrity means I am fair and just; I do not judge—oh Father, You must help me not to judge—and I look out for the interests of others, putting their interests before my own. Let there be no reason for others to find fault in me. Most of all, please find me faithful to You. In the dear name of Jesus, amen.

271.

Then the presidents and princes sought to find occasion against Daniel concerning the kingdom; but they could find none occasion nor fault; forasmuch as he was faithful, neither was there any error or fault found in him.

DANIEL 6:4

272.

And as for me, thou upholdest me in mine
integrity, and settest me before thy face for ever.

PSALM 41:12

273.

And the man said unto Joab, Though I should
receive a thousand shekels of silver in mine
hand, yet would I not put forth mine hand
against the king's son: for in our hearing the
king charged thee and Abishai and Ittai,
saying, Beware that none touch the young
man Absalom. Otherwise I should have
wrought falsehood against mine own life: for
there is no matter hid from the king, and thou
thyself wouldest have set thyself against me.

2 SAMUEL 18:12–13

274.

The just man walketh in his integrity:
his children are blessed after him.

PROVERBS 20:7

275.

The integrity of the upright shall
guide them: but the perverseness of
transgressors shall destroy them.

PROVERBS 11:3

⌒⌒⌒⌒⌒⌒⌒

276.

Better is the poor that walketh
in his integrity, than he that is
perverse in his lips, and is a fool.

PROVERBS 19:1

⌒⌒⌒⌒⌒⌒⌒

277.

Moreover they reckoned not with the men, into
whose hand they delivered the money to be
bestowed on workmen: for they dealt faithfully.

2 KINGS 12:15

278.

And he said unto him, Well, thou good servant:
because thou hast been faithful in a very little,
have thou authority over ten cities.

LUKE 19:17

279.

Moreover it is required in stewards,
that a man be found faithful.

1 CORINTHIANS 4:2

280.

Receive us; we have wronged no man, we have
corrupted no man, we have defrauded no man.

2 CORINTHIANS 7:2

JOY

Lord, what is joy? When did You experience it? Surely being a "man of sorrows" You did not feel joy all the time. You even wept. Did Your tears flow from the pain and brokenness of this world? We weep too, and we don't always know why. But You promise joy in the morning. Your joy is our strength. It's what Nehemiah told the people when their enemies were coming against them. And it's what You tell us when our enemies are coming against us. The greatest joy of all is the news the angels gave—that You, our Savior, would be born. For us it is, and for You? When we believe in You. In Your joyful name, amen.

281.

Behold, God is my salvation; I will trust, and not be afraid: for the LORD JEHOVAH is my strength and my song; he also is become my salvation. Therefore with joy shall ye draw water out of the wells of salvation.

ISAIAH 12:2–3

282.

And the angel said unto them, Fear not: for, behold, I bring you good tidings of great joy, which shall be to all people. For unto you is born this day in the city of David a Saviour, which is Christ the Lord.

Luke 2:10–11

283.

Thou wilt shew me the path of life: in thy presence is fulness of joy; at thy right hand there are pleasures for evermore.

Psalm 16:11

284.

For his anger endureth but a moment; in his favor is life: weeping may endure for a night, but joy cometh in the morning.

Psalm 30:5

285.

For the joy of the LORD is your strength.

NEHEMIAH 8:10

286.

What man of you, having an hundred sheep, if he lose one of them, doth not leave the ninety and nine in the wilderness, and go after that which is lost, until he find it? And when he hath found it, he layeth it on his shoulders, rejoicing. And when he cometh home, he calleth together his friends and neighbours, saying unto them, Rejoice with me; for I have found my sheep which was lost. I say unto you, that likewise joy shall be in heaven over one sinner that repenteth, more than over ninety and nine just persons, which need no repentance.

LUKE 15:4–7

287.

They that sow in tears shall reap in joy.

PSALM 126:5

288.
When they saw the star, they
rejoiced with exceeding great joy.

MATTHEW 2:10

289.
These things have I spoken unto you,
that my joy might remain in you,
and that your joy might be full.

JOHN 15:11

290.
And now come I to thee; and these things
I speak in the world, that they might
have my joy fulfilled in themselves.

JOHN 17:13

KINDNESS

*Lord, may I be as the woman of Proverbs who
spoke words of kindness to those around her. May
I not only speak kindness, but show kindness
as Boaz did for Ruth when he made sure she had
enough to glean. As David did for Jonathan's
son, who was lame. Too often, Lord, I am like
those who passed by the poor man beaten and
left to die by the roadside and not often enough
like the Samaritan who stopped to help him.
Help me to be kind to those around me—as You
are always kind to me. In Your name, amen.*

291.

And David said, Is there yet any that is left
of the house of Saul, that I may shew him
kindness for Jonathan's sake? . . . And Ziba
said unto the king, Jonathan hath yet a son,
which is lame on his feet. . . . And David said
unto him, Fear not: for I will surely shew thee
kindness for Jonathan thy father's sake, and will
restore thee all the land of Saul thy father; and
thou shalt eat bread at my table continually.

2 SAMUEL 9:1, 3, 7

292.

Now therefore fear ye not: I will nourish you,
and your little ones. And he comforted them,
and spake kindly unto them.

GENESIS 50:21

293.

And the shepherds came and drove
them away: but Moses stood up and
helped them, and watered their flock.

EXODUS 2:17

294.

And when she was risen up to glean, Boaz
commanded his young men, saying, Let her
glean even among the sheaves, and reproach
her not: and let fall also some of the handfuls
of purpose for her, and leave them, that she
may glean them, and rebuke her not.

RUTH 2:15–16

295.

She openeth her mouth with wisdom;
and in her tongue is the law of kindness.

PROVERBS 31:26

296.

But a certain Samaritan, as he journeyed, came
where he was: and when he saw him, he had
compassion on him, and went to him, and
bound up his wounds, pouring in oil and wine,
and set him on his own beast, and brought
him to an inn, and took care of him.

LUKE 10:33–34

297.

And the barbarous people shewed us no
little kindness: for they kindled a fire,
and received us every one, because of the
present rain, and because of the cold.

ACTS 28:2

298.

Be kindly affectioned one to another
with brotherly love; in honour
preferring one another.

ROMANS 12:10

299.

Charity suffereth long, and is kind.

1 CORINTHIANS 13:4

300.

Put on therefore, as the elect of God, holy
and beloved, bowels of mercies, kindness,
humbleness of mind, meekness, longsuffering.

COLOSSIANS 3:12

LOVE FOR OTHERS

*Father, teach me to love others as You love me.
They will know I belong to You if I love them.
But how do I love a difficult person? A family
member who has shown only hate? Someone
who curses me when I stand up for what is
right? Or a neighbor who puts trash in my
yard? You didn't say it would be easy to love
everyone. You just said to do it and You would
help me. Pretending to love someone won't
suffice either. You know my heart. If I have
hidden resentment or bad feelings toward
someone, please heal my heart so I may
serve You by loving others sincerely.
In Jesus' name, amen.*

301.

A new commandment I give unto you,
That ye love one another; as I have loved
you, that ye also love one another. By this
shall all men know that ye are my disciples,
if ye have love one to another.

JOHN 13:34–35

302.

And though I bestow all my goods to feed the poor, and though I give my body to be burned, and have not charity, it profiteth me nothing. Charity suffereth long, and is kind; charity envieth not; charity vaunteth not itself, is not puffed up, doth not behave itself unseemly, seeketh not her own, is not easily provoked, thinketh no evil; rejoiceth not in iniquity, but rejoiceth in the truth; beareth all things, believeth all things, hopeth all things, endureth all things. Charity never faileth.

1 CORINTHIANS 13:3–8

303.

But as touching brotherly love ye need not that I write unto you: for ye yourselves are taught of God to love one another.

1 THESSALONIANS 4:9

304.

Let brotherly love continue.

HEBREWS 13:1

305.

Brethren, ye have been called unto liberty;
only use not liberty for an occasion to the
flesh, but by love serve one another. For all
the law is fulfilled in one word, even in this;
Thou shalt love thy neighbour as thyself.

GALATIANS 5:13–14

306.

Wherefore I also, after I heard of your faith
in the Lord Jesus, and love unto all the
saints, cease not to give thanks for you,
making mention of you in my prayers.

EPHESIANS 1:15–16

307.

And the Lord make you to increase and abound
in love one toward another, and toward all
men, even as we do toward you.

1 THESSALONIANS 3:12

308.

Seeing ye have purified your souls in obeying the truth through the Spirit unto unfeigned love of the brethren, see that ye love one another with a pure heart fervently.

1 Peter 1:22

309.

And above all things have fervent charity among yourselves: for charity shall cover the multitude of sins.

1 Peter 4:8

310.

If a man say, I love God, and hateth his brother, he is a liar: for he that loveth not his brother whom he hath seen, how can he love God whom he hath not seen? And this commandment have we from him, That he who loveth God love his brother also.

1 John 4:20–21

MEEKNESS

Do I want to be meek, Lord? Do You really want me to be? The world seems to look at meekness as a bad quality—as if a meek person is someone to be walked on. But Your Word says the opposite: "The meek shall inherit the earth." That certainly isn't a bad thing, Lord. And even in the world's eyes inheriting the earth would be a mark of great favor. More than that, Lord, a meek and quiet spirit is of great worth to You. Please help me put Your favor above everyone else's and instill meekness within. Thank You, Lord.

311.

Put them in mind to be subject to principalities and powers, to obey magistrates, to be ready to every good work, to speak evil of no man, to be no brawlers, but gentle, shewing all meekness unto all men.

Titus 3:1–2

312.

But the meek shall inherit the earth;
and shall delight themselves
in the abundance of peace.

PSALM 37:11

313.

The meek also shall increase their joy in
the LORD, and the poor among men shall
rejoice in the Holy One of Israel.

ISAIAH 29:19

314.

Seek ye the LORD, all ye meek of the earth,
which have wrought his judgment; seek
righteousness, seek meekness: It may be ye
shall be hid in the day of the LORD's anger.

ZEPHANIAH 2:3

315.
Blessed are the meek:
for they shall inherit the earth.

MATTHEW 5:5

316.
Now I Paul myself beseech you by
the meekness and gentleness of Christ,
who in presence am base among you,
but being absent am bold toward you.

2 CORINTHIANS 10:1

317.
Brethren, if a man be overtaken in a fault,
ye which are spiritual, restore such an one
in the spirit of meekness; considering
thyself, lest thou also be tempted.

GALATIANS 6:1

318.
But the fruit of the Spirit is. . .meekness.

GALATIANS 5:22–23

319.
Who is a wise man and endued with
knowledge among you? Let him shew
out of a good conversation his works
with meekness of wisdom.

JAMES 3:13

320.
Let it be the hidden man of the heart,
in that which is not corruptible, even
the ornament of a meek and quiet spirit,
which is in the sight of God of great price.

1 PETER 3:4

MERCY

Father, You are full of mercy. You extend Your hand to me when I fall. You pick me up and set me back on my feet. Even when I fail You, Lord, You do not fail me. Thank You for not giving me what I deserve and for giving me what I do not deserve. All because of Your Son, Jesus. You see me through His death and resurrection. Great is Your faithfulness, Lord God. I stand in awe of You. Your mercy is new every morning when I awaken. I do not always sense it, but You give it freely. Please write mercy on my heart that I may share it with those around me. In Jesus' name, amen.

321.

(For the LORD thy God is a merciful God;)
he will not forsake thee, neither destroy
thee, nor forget the covenant of thy
fathers which he sware unto them.

DEUTERONOMY 4:31

322.

And David said unto Gad, I am in a great
strait: let us fall now into the hand of the
LORD; for his mercies are great: and let
me not fall into the hand of man.

2 SAMUEL 24:14

323.

For thou, Lord, art good, and ready
to forgive; and plenteous in mercy
unto all them that call upon thee.

PSALM 86:5

324.

For a small moment have I forsaken thee;
but with great mercies will I gather thee.
In a little wrath I hid my face from
thee for a moment; but with everlasting
kindness will I have mercy on thee,
saith the LORD thy Redeemer.

ISAIAH 54:7–8

325.

Let not mercy and truth forsake thee:
bind them about thy neck; write them
upon the table of thine heart: so shalt
thou find favour and good understanding
in the sight of God and man.

PROVERBS 3:3–4

326.

Praise ye the LORD. O give thanks
unto the LORD; for he is good:
for his mercy endureth for ever.

PSALM 106:1

327.

It is of the LORD's mercies that we are
not consumed, because his compassions
fail not. They are new every morning:
great is thy faithfulness.

LAMENTATIONS 3:22–23

328.
Blessed are the merciful:
for they shall obtain mercy.

MATTHEW 5:7

329.
Be ye therefore merciful,
as your Father also is merciful.

LUKE 6:36

330.
Not by works of righteousness which we have
done, but according to his mercy he saved us,
by the washing of regeneration, and renewing
of the Holy Ghost; which he shed on us
abundantly through Jesus Christ our Saviour.

TITUS 3:5–6

OBEDIENCE

Father, You desire my obedience. But I don't always want to obey. I think I know what's best when facing multiple choices. Yet I must remember You created me and know me through and through. I can make no better choice than to follow You with my whole heart. When the ways of the world conflict with Your ways, help me choose to obey You rather than the world. Please nudge me onto the clear path You have laid out for me. Your Son chose obedience to You—the cross—rather than His own way. Too often I have failed when I haven't obeyed You. You would have me find success though, not failure. Your Word always leads me to You, the best choice. Thank You, Father.

331.

Now therefore, if ye will obey my voice indeed, and keep my covenant, then ye shall be a peculiar treasure unto me above all people: for all the earth is mine.

Exodus 19:5

332.

This book of the law shall not depart out of
thy mouth; but thou shalt meditate therein
day and night, that thou mayest observe to
do according to all that is written therein:
for then thou shalt make thy way prosperous,
and then thou shalt have good success.

JOSHUA 1:8

333.

And Samuel said, Hath the LORD as great
delight in burnt offerings and sacrifices,
as in obeying the voice of the LORD? Behold,
to obey is better than sacrifice, and to
hearken than the fat of rams. For rebellion
is as the sin of witchcraft, and stubbornness
is as iniquity and idolatry. Because thou hast
rejected the word of the LORD, he hath also
rejected thee from being king.

1 SAMUEL 15:22–23

334.

When thou saidst, Seek ye my face; my heart
said unto thee, Thy face, LORD, will I seek.

PSALM 27:8

335.

But this thing commanded I them, saying,
Obey my voice, and I will be your God, and
ye shall be my people: and walk ye in all the
ways that I have commanded you, that it may
be well unto you. But they hearkened not, nor
inclined their ear, but walked in the counsels
and in the imagination of their evil heart,
and went backward, and not forward.

JEREMIAH 7:23–24

336.

Not every one that saith unto me, Lord,
Lord, shall enter into the kingdom of
heaven; but he that doeth the will of
my Father which is in heaven.

MATTHEW 7:21

337.

And the disciples went, and
did as Jesus commanded them.

MATTHEW 21:6

338.

And when they had brought them, they set them before the council: and the high priest asked them, saying, Did not we straitly command you that ye should not teach in this name? and, behold, ye have filled Jerusalem with your doctrine, and intend to bring this man's blood upon us. Then Peter and the other apostles answered and said, We ought to obey God rather than men.

ACTS 5:27–29

339.

Children, obey your parents in all things: for this is well pleasing unto the Lord.

COLOSSIANS 3:20

340.

Though he were a Son, yet learned he obedience by the things which he suffered; and being made perfect, he became the author of eternal salvation unto all them that obey him.

HEBREWS 5:8–9

PATIENCE

Oh Lord, You want me to be patient with everyone? How is that possible? Doesn't that seem like a stretch? I'm not even patient with myself. And waiting for an answer from You is difficult at best sometimes. Couldn't I be more like the psalmist, whose soul waited for You more than those who watch for the sun to rise? You want me to rest and wait patiently. Perhaps the key is resting in You. That would be so wonderful, such a relief, to know I can rest in Your arms and wait for You to work out things. Please help me find that place of rest in You and extend Your patience to others. In Your name, amen.

341.

I wait for the LORD, my soul doth wait, and in his word do I hope. My soul waiteth for the Lord more than they that watch for the morning; I say, more than they that watch for the morning.

PSALM 130:5–6

342.
I have waited for thy salvation, O LORD.

GENESIS 49:18

343.
Rest in the LORD, and wait patiently for him; fret not thyself because of him who prospereth in his way, because of the man who bringeth wicked devices to pass.

PSALM 37:7

344.
Better is the end of a thing than the beginning thereof: and the patient in spirit is better than the proud in spirit.

ECCLESIASTES 7:8

345.

The LORD is good unto them that wait for him, to the soul that seeketh him.

LAMENTATIONS 3:25

346.

Be patient toward all men.

1 THESSALONIANS 5:14

347.

And the servant of the Lord must not strive: but be gentle unto all men, apt to teach, patient.

2 TIMOTHY 2:24

348.

And so, after he had patiently endured,
he obtained the promise.

HEBREWS 6:15

349.

For ye have need of patience, that,
after ye have done the will of God,
ye might receive the promise.

HEBREWS 10:36

350.

But let patience have her perfect
work, that ye may be perfect and
entire, wanting nothing.

JAMES 1:4

PEACE

What amazing peace You offer, Lord. Perfect peace when my thoughts focus on You. Elusive peace when I doubt and worry. Promised peace for You have overcome the world. You give me sweet sleep and safe dwelling—all I could ask for. When the world is in chaos and my neighbors are restless, help me remember who You are. Help me trust You with all my heart. Let me be glad and find peace when I see You. Help me live in harmony with those around me. Show us who You are—the Prince of Peace. In Your dear name, amen.

351.

Then the same day at evening, being the first day of the week, when the doors were shut where the disciples were assembled for fear of the Jews, came Jesus and stood in the midst, and saith unto them, Peace be unto you. And when he had so said, he shewed unto them his hands and his side. Then were the disciples glad, when they saw the Lord.

JOHN 20:19–20

352.

And suddenly there was with the angel a multitude of the heavenly host praising God, and saying, Glory to God in the highest, and on earth peace, good will toward men.

LUKE 2:13–14

353.

These things I have spoken unto you, that in me ye might have peace. In the world ye shall have tribulation: but be of good cheer; I have overcome the world.

JOHN 16:33

354.

Thou wilt keep him in perfect peace, whose mind is stayed on thee: because he trusteth in thee.

ISAIAH 26:3

355.

The LORD will give strength unto his people;
the LORD will bless his people with peace.

PSALM 29:11

356.

Peace I leave with you, my peace I
give unto you: not as the world giveth,
give I unto you. Let not your heart be
troubled, neither let it be afraid.

JOHN 14:27

357.

Great peace have they which love thy law:
and nothing shall offend them.

PSALM 119:165

358.

I will both lay me down in
peace, and sleep: for thou, LORD,
only makest me dwell in safety.

PSALM 4:8

359.

Finally, brethren, farewell. Be perfect,
be of good comfort, be of one mind,
live in peace; and the God of love
and peace shall be with you.

2 CORINTHIANS 13:11

360.

Now the Lord of peace himself give
you peace always by all means.
The Lord be with you all.

2 THESSALONIANS 3:16

PERSEVERANCE

Hang on, You say? How do I hang on when my life is spiraling out of control? When my ship is sinking? When it seems the world is against me? I guess You want me to hold on to what is good, Lord, to stay the course, to keep the faith. Your Word says that if I don't give up when I'm doing the right thing then I'll reap a good harvest. How long will it take? Will I see reconciliation in this life? Or must I wait for heaven? You endured the cross for us. Help me persevere in prayer, Lord, until the miracle comes. Only You can do it. Thank You.

361.

Wherefore seeing we also are compassed about with so great a cloud of witnesses, let us lay aside every weight, and the sin which doth so easily beset us, and let us run with patience the race that is set before us.

HEBREWS 12:1

362.

And he spake a parable unto them to this end, that men ought always to pray, and not to faint; saying, There was in a city a judge, which feared not God, neither regarded man: and there was a widow in that city; and she came unto him, saying, Avenge me of mine adversary. And he would not for a while: but afterward he said within himself, Though I fear not God, nor regard man; yet because this widow troubleth me, I will avenge her, lest by her continual coming she weary me. And the Lord said, Hear what the unjust judge saith. And shall not God avenge his own elect, which cry day and night unto him, though he bear long with them? I tell you that he will avenge them speedily. Nevertheless when the Son of man cometh, shall he find faith on the earth?

Luke 18:1–8

363.

And let us not be weary in well doing: for in due season we shall reap, if we faint not.

Galatians 6:9

364.

Now when the congregation was broken up, many of the Jews and religious proselytes followed Paul and Barnabas: who, speaking to them, persuaded them to continue in the grace of God.

ACTS 13:43

365.

But continue thou in the things which thou hast learned and hast been assured of, knowing of whom thou hast learned them.

2 TIMOTHY 3:14

366.

The righteous also shall hold on his way, and he that hath clean hands shall be stronger and stronger.

JOB 17:9

367.

Behold, I come quickly: hold that fast which thou hast, that no man take thy crown.

REVELATION 3:11

368.

Looking unto Jesus the author and finisher
of our faith; who for the joy that was set
before him endured the cross, despising
the shame, and is set down at the right
hand of the throne of God.

HEBREWS 12:2

369.

Wherefore gird up the loins of your mind,
be sober, and hope to the end for the grace
that is to be brought unto you at the
revelation of Jesus Christ.

1 PETER 1:13

370.

And I heard a loud voice saying in heaven, Now
is come salvation, and strength, and the kingdom of our God, and the power of his Christ:
for the accuser of our brethren is cast down,
which accused them before our God day and
night. And they overcame him by the blood of
the Lamb, and by the word of their testimony;
and they loved not their lives unto the death.

REVELATION 12:10–11

PRAISE

You alone are worthy of praise, Lord God.
You have redeemed me from my sin. You have
brought me out of the darkness into a life
shining brightly with Your light and truth. You
have taken my guilt and washed me white as
snow. One day every creature will sing Your
praises. One day everyone will acknowledge
You as Lord. As long as I have breath, may
I praise You. I will think on You and Your
wonderful gifts to me, and I will sing praise to
You. Even when I feel alone, I will praise
You, the One who loves me more than anyone
else can. In the name of Jesus, amen.

371.

And they, continuing daily with one accord in
the temple, and breaking bread from house to
house, did eat their meat with gladness and
singleness of heart, praising God, and having
favor with all the people. And the Lord added
to the church daily such as should be saved.

Acts 2:46–47

372.

Sing, O heavens; and be joyful, O earth;
and break forth into singing, O mountains:
for the LORD hath comforted his people,
and will have mercy upon his afflicted.

ISAIAH 49:13

373.

But ye are a chosen generation, a royal priest-
hood, a holy nation, a peculiar people; that ye
should shew forth the praises of him who hath
called you out of darkness into his marvellous
light: which in time past were not a people,
but are now the people of God: which had not
obtained mercy, but now have obtained mercy.

1 PETER 2:9–10

374.

Let everything that hath breath praise
the LORD. Praise ye the LORD.

PSALM 150:6

375.

And every creature which is in heaven, and on the earth, and under the earth, and such as are in the sea, and all that are in them, heard I saying, Blessing, and honor, and glory, and power, be unto him that sitteth upon the throne, and unto the Lamb for ever and ever.

REVELATION 5:13

376.

And the shepherds returned, glorifying and praising God for all the things that they had heard and seen, as it was told unto them.

LUKE 2:20

377.

O Lord, open thou my lips; and my mouth shall shew forth thy praise.

PSALM 51:15

378.

By him therefore let us offer the sacrifice of praise to God continually, that is, the fruit of our lips giving thanks to his name.

HEBREWS 13:15

379.

I will sing unto the LORD as long as I live: I will sing praise to my God while I have my being. My meditation of him shall be sweet: I will be glad in the LORD.

PSALM 104:33–34

380.

Let the people praise thee, O God; let all the people praise thee.

PSALM 67:3

PRAYER

*Sometimes the only thing we can do is pray,
Father, when troubles come. Is it for our
benefit that You want us to pray? How does
it change things? When we don't pray, do You
still work things out on our behalf? When we
are so deeply mired in a problem and cannot
pray, do You still answer what is hidden in our
hearts? You heal through prayer. You cause the
rain to stop and start by prayer. Your Son prays
for us. Your Spirit prays even now for us in a
way we cannot understand. He intercedes on
our behalf, according to Your will. Teach us to
pray, Father. O teach us to pray.*

381.

And the king answered and said unto the
man of God, Intreat now the face of the Lord
thy God, and pray for me, that my hand may
be restored me again. And the man of God
besought the Lord, and the king's hand was
restored him again, and became as it was before.

1 Kings 13:6

382.

Seek the LORD and his strength,
seek his face continually.

1 CHRONICLES 16:11

383.

And it came to pass, that, as he was praying
in a certain place, when he ceased, one of
his disciples said unto him, Lord, teach us to
pray, as John also taught his disciples. And he
said unto them, When ye pray, say, Our Father
which art in heaven. Hallowed be thy name. Thy
kingdom come. Thy will be done, as in heaven,
so in earth. Give us day by day our daily bread.
And forgive us our sins; for we also forgive every
one that is indebted to us. And lead us not into
temptation, but deliver us from evil.

LUKE 11:1–4

384.

Therefore I will look unto the LORD;
I will wait for the God of my salvation:
my God will hear me.

MICAH 7:7

385.

Even them will I bring to my holy mountain,
and make them joyful in my house of prayer:
their burnt offerings and their sacrifices shall be
accepted upon mine altar; for mine house shall
be called a house of prayer for all people.

Isaiah 56:7

386.

Watch ye therefore, and pray always,
that ye may be accounted worthy to
escape all these things that shall come to
pass, and to stand before the Son of man.

Luke 21:36

387.

These words spake Jesus, and lifted up his eyes
to heaven, and said, Father, the hour is come;
glorify thy Son, that thy Son also may glorify
thee: as thou hast given him power over all
flesh, that he should give eternal life to as many
as thou hast given him. And this is life eternal,
that they might know thee the only true God,
and Jesus Christ, whom thou hast sent.

John 17:1–3

388.

Likewise the Spirit also helpeth our infirmities: for we know not what we should pray for as we ought: but the Spirit itself maketh intercession for us with groanings which cannot be uttered. And he that searcheth the hearts knoweth what is the mind of the Spirit, because he maketh intercession for the saints according to the will of God.

ROMANS 8:26–27

389.

Pray without ceasing.

1 THESSALONIANS 5:17

390.

Confess your faults one to another, and pray one for another, that ye may be healed. The effectual fervent prayer of a righteous man availeth much. Elias was a man subject to like passions as we are, and he prayed earnestly that it might not rain: and it rained not on the earth by the space of three years and six months. And he prayed again, and the heaven gave rain, and the earth brought forth her fruit.

JAMES 5:16–18

REPENTANCE

Merciful Father, You have promised to forgive our sins and heal our land when we repent and turn to You. Peter wept with sorrow when he realized he had denied Your Son, just as it was foretold him. The prodigal son came home with repentance in his heart, in his words, and in his deeds, and his father ran to meet him. In the same way You welcome us when we come home to You in true repentance. You rejoice with the angels in heaven when only one person changes direction and follows after You. Guide us to our knees. Heal us and bring refreshing to our land. In Jesus' name, amen.

391.

Yet the LORD testified against Israel, and against Judah, by all the prophets, and by all the seers, saying, Turn ye from your evil ways, and keep my commandments and my statutes, according to all the law which I commanded your father, and which I sent to you by my servants the prophets.

2 KINGS 17:13

392.

If my people, which are called by my name,
shall humble themselves, and pray, and seek
my face, and turn from their wicked ways;
then will I hear from heaven, and will forgive
their sin, and will heal their land.

2 CHRONICLES 7:14

393.

They said, Turn ye again now every one from
his evil way, and from the evil of your doings,
and dwell in the land that the LORD hath given
unto you and to your fathers for ever and ever.

JEREMIAH 25:5

394.

Wherefore, O king, let my counsel be
acceptable unto thee, and break off thy
sins by righteousness, and thine iniquities
by shewing mercy to the poor; if it may
be a lengthening of thy tranquility.

DANIEL 4:27

395.

In those days came John the Baptist, preaching
in the wilderness of Judea, and saying, Repent
ye: for the kingdom of heaven is at hand.

MATTHEW 3:1–2

396.

And the second time the cock crew. And
Peter called to mind the word that Jesus
said unto him, Before the cock crow
twice, thou shalt deny me thrice. And
when he thought thereon, he wept.

MARK 14:72

397.

I say unto you, that likewise joy shall be
in heaven over one sinner that repenteth,
more than over ninety and nine just persons,
which need no repentance.

LUKE 15:7

398.

And he arose, and came to his father. But when he was yet a great way off, his father saw him, and had compassion, and ran, and fell on his neck, and kissed him. And the son said unto him, Father, I have sinned against heaven, and in thy sight, and am no more worthy to be called thy son. But the father said to his servants, Bring forth the best robe, and put it on him; and put a ring on his hand, and shoes on his feet. . . . For this my son was dead, and is alive again; he was lost, and is found.

LUKE 15:20–22, 24

399.

Then Peter said unto them, Repent, and be baptized every one of you in the name of Jesus Christ for the remission of sins, and ye shall receive the gift of the Holy Ghost.

ACTS 2:38

400.

Repent ye therefore, and be converted, that your sins may be blotted out, when the times of refreshing shall come from the presence of the Lord.

ACTS 3:19

REST

Father, You know our need for rest. Though nothing tires You out, You chose to rest after creating the world and all that is in it. You are our example when we think we must keep working until the sun goes down and the moon comes up. You have created within us a need for rest. And You have promised to be with us and meet that need. Our hearts long for another kind of rest in the midst of this troubled world. Please, Father, lead us beside still waters and help us find our rest by faith in You alone. Amen.

401.

There remaineth therefore a rest to the people of God. For he that is entered into his rest, he also hath ceased from his own works, as God did from his. Let us labour therefore to enter into that rest, lest any man fall after the same example of unbelief.

HEBREWS 4:9–11.

402.

Six days thou shalt do thy work, and on the
seventh day thou shalt rest: that thine ox
and thine ass may rest, and the son of thy
handmaid, and the stranger, may be refreshed.

Exodus 23:12

403.

And he said, My presence shall go
with thee, and I will give thee rest.

Exodus 33:14

404.

And he said unto them, Come ye yourselves
apart into a desert place, and rest a while: for
there were many coming and going, and they
had no leisure so much as to eat. And they
departed into a desert place by ship privately.

Mark 6:31–32

405.

And I said, Oh that I had wings like a dove!
for then would I fly away, and be at rest.

PSALM 55:6

406.

Take my yoke upon you, and learn of me;
for I am meek and lowly in heart: and ye
shall find rest unto your souls. For my
yoke is easy, and my burden is light.

MATTHEW 11:29–30

407.

For thus saith the Lord GOD, the Holy One of
Israel: In returning and rest shall ye be saved;
in quietness and in confidence shall be
your strength: and ye would not.

ISAIAH 30:15

408.

Return unto thy rest, O my soul; for the
LORD hath dealt bountifully with thee.

PSALM 116:7

409.

He maketh me to lie down in green pastures:
he leadeth me beside the still waters.

PSALM 23:2

410.

And on the seventh day God ended
his work which he had made; and he
rested on the seventh day from all
his work which he had made.

GENESIS 2:2

SCRIPTURE

*Thank You for Your Word, Lord, a lamp for
my feet and a light on my path. Thank You for
giving me written words that I may turn to when
I feel lost in the dark, not knowing which way to
go. Dependable. Pure. Trustworthy. These words
describe Your Word. I can never go wrong when
I follow You. My faith grows when I hear Your
Word. You give me understanding through Your
Spirit living inside me. My heart burns within
me when You open the Scriptures to me, when
You reveal the truth. Please open my eyes to see
You. In Your dear name, amen.*

411.

The law of the LORD is perfect, converting the
soul: the testimony of the LORD is sure, making
wise the simple. The statutes of the LORD are
right, rejoicing the heart: the commandment of
the LORD is pure, enlightening the eyes.

PSALM 19:7–8

412.

As for God, his way is perfect: the word
of the LORD is tried: he is a buckler
to all those that trust in him.

PSALM 18:30

413.

The words of the LORD are pure
words: as silver tried in a furnace
of earth, purified seven times.

PSALM 12:6

414.

Search the scriptures; for in them ye
think ye have eternal life: and they are
they which testify of me. And ye will not
come to me, that ye might have life.

JOHN 5:39–40

415.

Jesus answered and said unto them,
Ye do err, not knowing the scriptures,
nor the power of God.

MATTHEW 22:29

416.

And they said one to another, Did not our heart
burn within us, while he talked with us by the
way, and while he opened to us the scriptures?

LUKE 24:32

417.

Men and brethren, this scripture must
needs have been fulfilled, which the
Holy Ghost by the mouth of David spake
before concerning Judas, which was
guide to them that took Jesus.

ACTS 1:16

418.

Thy word is a lamp unto my feet,
and a light unto my path.

PSALM 119:105

419.

Wherefore, beloved, seeing that ye look
for such things, be diligent that ye may be
found of him in peace, without spot, and
blameless. And account that the longsuffering
of our Lord is salvation; even as our beloved
brother Paul also according to the wisdom
given unto him hath written unto you; as also
in all his epistles, speaking in them of these
things; in which are some things hard to be
understood, which they that are unlearned
and unstable wrest, as they do also the other
scriptures, unto their own destruction.

2 PETER 3:14–16

420.

If ye fulfil the royal law according to
the scripture, Thou shalt love thy
neighbour as thyself, ye do well.

JAMES 2:8

SELF-CONTROL

Father, You know the areas of my life where I struggle with self-control. I've tried to shore up the weak places in my lifestyle. I've asked for Your help so many times. But why do I have to work so hard at it when self-control is a fruit of Your Spirit within me? When I'm failing again and again, does that mean I don't have Your Spirit? I need self-control in so many ways: being slow to get angry, not judging others, not gossiping, managing my time and my health. Help me see Your Spirit at work in me, teaching me self-control in all areas. Thank You, Father.

421.

And every man that striveth for the mastery is temperate in all things. Now they do it to obtain a corruptible crown; but we an incorruptible. I therefore so run, not as uncertainly; so fight I, not as one that beateth the air: but I keep under my body, and bring it into subjection: lest that by any means, when I have preached to others, I myself should be a castaway.

1 Corinthians 9:25–27

422.

He that hath no rule over his own spirit is like
a city that is broken down, and without walls.

PROVERBS 25:28

423.

But they said, We will drink no wine:
for Jonadab the son of Rechab our father
commanded us, saying, Ye shall drink no
wine, neither ye, nor your sons for ever.

JEREMIAH 35:6

424.

But Daniel purposed in his heart that he would
not defile himself with the portion of the
king's meat, nor with the wine which he drank:
therefore he requested of the prince of the
eunuchs that he might not defile himself.

DANIEL 1:8

425.

Let not sin therefore reign in your mortal body,
that ye should obey it in the lusts thereof.

ROMANS 6:12

426.

All things are lawful unto me, but all things are
not expedient: all things are lawful for me, but
I will not be brought under the power of any.

1 CORINTHIANS 6:12

427.

He that is slow to anger is better than
the mighty; and he that ruleth his
spirit than he that taketh a city.

PROVERBS 16:32

428.

But the fruit of the Spirit is. . .temperance:
against such there is no law.

GALATIANS 5:22–23

429.

For in many things we offend all. If any man
offend not in word, the same is a perfect man,
and able also to bridle the whole body. . . .
But the tongue can no man tame; it is an
unruly evil, full of deadly poison.

JAMES 3:2, 8

430.

And besides this, giving all diligence,
add to your faith virtue; and to virtue
knowledge; and to knowledge temperance;
and to temperance patience; and to patience
godliness; and to godliness brotherly
kindness; and to brotherly kindness charity.

2 PETER 1:5–7

SIN, FREEDOM FROM

What a relief it is to know, Lord, that You have set me free from sin! You never had to deal with that. But it is something we all must face as humans who have a knack for making bad choices. We were born in sin, and our natural proclivity is to sin, to put ourselves above You, to miss the mark You have set. We were held captive to sin, but You set us free. Believing in You gives us the freedom for which we long. We are no longer servants of sin but servants of righteousness. We serve You, the living God. Help us serve one another in love that all may be set free. In Your name, amen.

431.
The Spirit of the Lord GOD is upon me; because the LORD hath anointed me to preach good tidings unto the meek; he hath sent me to bind up the brokenhearted, to proclaim liberty to the captives, and the opening of the prison to them that are bound.

ISAIAH 61:1

432.

Then said Jesus to those Jews which believed
on him, If ye continue in my word, then are
ye my disciples indeed; and ye shall know the
truth, and the truth shall make you free.

JOHN 8:31–32

433.

But take heed lest by any means
this liberty of yours become a
stumblingblock to them that are weak.

1 CORINTHIANS 8:9

434.

Let not sin therefore reign in your mortal body,
that ye should obey it in the lusts thereof. . . .
For sin shall not have dominion over you: for
ye are not under the law, but under grace. . . .
But God be thanked, that ye were the servants
of sin, but ye have obeyed from the heart that
form of doctrine which was delivered you.
Being then made free from sin, ye became
the servants of righteousness.

ROMANS 6:12, 14, 17–18

435.

Because the creature itself also shall be delivered from the bondage of corruption into the glorious liberty of the children of God.

ROMANS 8:21

436.

Jesus answered them, Verily, verily, I say unto you, Whosoever committeth sin is the servant of sin. . . . If the Son therefore shall make you free, ye shall be free indeed.

JOHN 8:34, 36

437.

And that because of false brethren unawares brought in, who came in privily to spy out our liberty which we have in Christ Jesus, that they might bring us into bondage: to whom we gave place by subjection, no, not for an hour; that the truth of the gospel might continue with you.

GALATIANS 2:4–5

438.

For the law of the Spirit of life in Christ
Jesus hath made me free from
the law of sin and death.

ROMANS 8:2

439.

For, brethren, ye have been called unto liberty;
only use not liberty for an occasion to the
flesh, but by love serve one another.

GALATIANS 5:13

440.

As free, and not using your liberty
for a cloak of maliciousness,
but as the servants of God.

1 PETER 2:16

TEMPTATION

Father, You have known from the beginning of time that we would face temptation. You gave us the example of Satan tempting Your Son in the wilderness. Jesus knew exactly what to say: He spoke the Word, and the devil gave up. That's our game plan. The devil comes, and we speak Your Word—and watch him flee. He seeks to entice us away from our faith in You. He wants us to doubt Your very existence. He wants us to forget You love us. He wants us to forget You! But You have given us a way to escape. Oh, that we may watch and pray, Father, and endure to the end. In Your precious Son's name, amen.

441.

There hath no temptation taken you but such as is common to man: but God is faithful, who will not suffer you to be tempted above that ye are able; but will with the temptation also make a way to escape, that ye may be able to bear it.

1 CORINTHIANS 10:13

442.

And Satan stood up against Israel and provoked David to number Israel.

1 Chronicles 21:1

443.

Then was Jesus led up of the spirit into the wilderness to be tempted of the devil. And when he had fasted forty days and forty nights, he was afterward an hungred. And when the tempter came to him, he said, If thou be the Son of God, command that these stones be made bread. But he answered and said, It is written, Man shall not live by bread alone, but by every word that proceedeth out of the mouth of God.

Matthew 4:1–4

444.

Watch and pray, that ye enter not into temptation; the spirit indeed is willing, but the flesh is weak.

Matthew 26:41

445.

To whom ye forgive any thing, I forgive also:
for if I forgave any thing, to whom I forgave
it, for your sakes forgave I it in the person of
Christ; lest Satan should get an advantage of
us; for we are not ignorant of his devices.

2 Corinthians 2:10–11

446.

For this cause, when I could no longer
forbear, I sent to know your faith, lest by
some means the tempter have tempted
you, and our labor be in vain.

1 Thessalonians 3:5

447.

For in that he himself hath suffered
being tempted, he is able to succor
them that are tempted.

Hebrews 2:18

448.

Blessed is the man that endureth temptation: for when he is tried, he shall receive the crown of life, which the Lord hath promised to them that love him. Let no man say when he is tempted, I am tempted of God: for God cannot be tempted with evil, neither tempteth he any man: But every man is tempted, when he is drawn away of his own lust, and enticed. Then when lust hath conceived, it bringeth forth sin: and sin, when it is finished, bringeth forth death.

JAMES 1:12–15

449.

Submit yourselves therefore to God.
Resist the devil, and he will flee from you.

JAMES 4:7

450.

Be sober, be vigilant; because your adversary the devil, as a roaring lion, walketh about, seeking whom he may devour; whom resist steadfast in the faith, knowing that the same afflictions are accomplished in your brethren that are in the world.

1 PETER 5:8–9

TRUST

It is so much better to trust in You, Lord, than to trust in myself or in others. You have never let me down. You have never failed me. But I have failed myself, and others have failed me too. When I am afraid, please help me trust in You. You lead me. You bring to pass all that You have promised. You surround me with mercy. Help me trust You with my whole heart. My hope is in You. When I doubt, help me trust. You know me. And You will keep what I have committed to You—my heart. In Your dear name, amen.

451.

They that trust in the LORD shall be as mount Zion, which cannot be removed, but abideth for ever. As the mountains are round about Jerusalem, so the LORD is round about his people from henceforth even for ever.

PSALM 125:1–2

452.

Trust in the LORD, and do good; so shalt thou
dwell in the land, and verily thou shalt be
fed. . . . Commit thy way unto the LORD;
trust also in him; and he shall bring it to pass.

PSALM 37:3, 5

453.

What time I am afraid, I will trust in thee.
In God I will praise his word, in God
I have put my trust; I will not fear
what flesh can do unto me.

PSALM 56:3–4

454.

I will say of the LORD, He is my refuge and
my fortress: my God; in him will I trust.

PSALM 91:2

455.

It is better to trust in the LORD than to put confidence in man. It is better to trust in the LORD than to put confidence in princes.

PSALM 118:8–9

456.

Many sorrows shall be to the wicked: but he that trusteth in the LORD, mercy shall compass him about.

PSALM 32:10

457.

Trust in the LORD with all thine heart; and lean not unto thine own understanding. In all thy ways acknowledge him, and he shall direct thy paths.

PROVERBS 3:5–6

458.

Blessed is the man that trusteth in the LORD,
and whose hope the LORD is.

JEREMIAH 17:7

———

459.

The LORD is good, a strong hold in
the day of trouble; and he knoweth
them that trust in him.

NAHUM 1:7

———

460.

For the which cause I also suffer these things:
nevertheless I am not ashamed: for I know
whom I have believed, and am persuaded
that he is able to keep that which I have
committed unto him against that day.

2 TIMOTHY 1:12

WISDOM

I need wisdom, Lord. Wisdom to make good decisions in my work, my plans, and my relationships—in every part of my life. You want me to be wise. Daniel knew You to be wise and fair and trusted You with his whole life. He saw Your power. He chose to obey You above the king and found wisdom for his daily life. To know You is the first step toward being wise. By wisdom You created the world and all that is therein. How can I find wisdom? By asking You and by reading and following Your Word. You will give me freely and gently all the wisdom I need. Thank You, Lord.

461.

But continue thou in the things which thou hast learned and hast been assured of, knowing of whom thou hast learned them; and that from a child thou hast known the holy scriptures, which are able to make thee wise unto salvation through faith which is in Christ Jesus.

2 Timothy 3:14–15

462.

The fear of the LORD is the beginning
of wisdom: a good understanding have
all they that do his commandments:
his praise endureth for ever.

PSALM 111:10

⟞————————————⟝

463.

Daniel answered and said, Blessed be the
name of God for ever and ever; for wisdom
and might are his: and he changeth the times
and the seasons: he removeth kings, and
setteth up kings: he giveth wisdom unto the
wise, and knowledge to them that know
understanding. He revealeth the deep and
secret things: he knoweth what is in the
darkness, and the light dwelleth with him.

DANIEL 2:20–22

⟞————————————⟝

464.

The LORD by wisdom hath founded
the earth; by understanding hath
he established the heavens.

PROVERBS 3:19

465.

And the spirit of the LORD shall rest upon him,
the spirit of wisdom and understanding,
the spirit of counsel and might, the spirit of
knowledge and of the fear of the LORD.

ISAIAH 11:2

466.

Wisdom is the principal thing:
therefore get wisdom; and with all
thy getting get understanding.

PROVERBS 4:7

467.

If any of you lack wisdom, let him ask of
God, that giveth to all men liberally, and
upbraideth not: and it shall be given him.
But let him ask in faith, nothing wavering.
For he that wavereth is like a wave of the
sea driven with the wind and tossed.

JAMES 1:5–6

468.

O the depth of the riches both of the wisdom
and knowledge of God! How unsearchable are
his judgments, and his ways past finding out!

ROMANS 11:33

469.

And unto man he said, Behold, the fear
of the LORD, that is wisdom; and to
depart from evil is understanding.

JOB 28:28

470.

But the wisdom that is from above is first
pure, then peaceable, gentle, and easy to be
entreated, full of mercy and good fruits,
without partiality, and without hypocrisy.

JAMES 3:17

WORRY

Fear and worry seem to go hand in hand, don't they, Lord? If I'm afraid, I worry. If I'm worried, I'm afraid. But You don't want me to entertain these emotions. They creep into my thoughts and actions so easily. Help me to capture my thoughts, Lord. Time and time again I've seen that worrying does no good. You said it wouldn't, so why do I return to it so often? I strive to control my circumstances, but ultimately I have no power over so many things. You do though. You know my needs, and You meet them. You are the strength of my heart. Help me bring every care, every concern, to You in prayer— and there will I find peace. Trusting in Your name, amen.

471.

Fret not thyself because of evildoers, neither be thou envious against the workers of iniquity. For they shall soon be cut down like the grass, and wither as the green herb.

Psalm 37:1–2

472.

I will not be afraid of ten thousands
of people that have set themselves
against me round about.

PSALM 3:6

473.

The LORD is my light and my salvation;
whom shall I fear? The LORD is the strength of
my life; of whom shall I be afraid? . . . Though
a host should encamp against me, my heart
shall not fear: though war should rise against
me, in this will I be confident. One thing have I
desired of the LORD, that will I seek after: that I
may dwell in the house of the LORD all the days
of my life, to behold the beauty of the LORD,
and to inquire in his temple.

PSALM 27:1, 3–4

474.

And when Saul saw the host of the Philistines,
he was afraid, and his heart greatly trembled.

1 SAMUEL 28:5

475.

Thou shalt not be afraid for the terror by night;
nor for the arrow that flieth by day; nor for the
pestilence that walketh in darkness; nor for
the destruction that wasteth at noonday.

Psalm 91:5–6

476.

Therefore I say unto you, Take no thought for
your life, what ye shall eat, or what ye shall
drink; nor yet for your body, what ye shall put
on. Is not the life more than meat, and the
body than raiment? Behold the fowls of the
air: for they sow not, neither do they reap, nor
gather into barns; yet your heavenly Father
feedeth them. Are ye not much better than they?

Matthew 6:25–26

477.

Take therefore no thought for the morrow: for
the morrow shall take thought for the things of
itself. Sufficient unto the day is the evil thereof.

Matthew 6:34

478.

Therefore take no thought, saying, What shall we eat? Or, What shall we drink: or, Wherewithal shall we be clothed? (For after all these things do the Gentiles seek:) for your heavenly Father knoweth that he have need of all these things.

MATTHEW 6:31–32

479.

But Martha was cumbered about much serving, and came to him, and said, Lord, dost thou not care that my sister hath left me to serve alone? Bid her therefore that she help me. And Jesus answered and said unto her, Martha, Martha, thou art careful and troubled about many things: but one thing is needful: and Mary hath chosen that good part, which shall not be taken away from her.

LUKE 10:40–42

480.

Be careful for nothing; but in every thing by prayer and supplication with thanksgiving let your requests be made known unto God. And the peace of God, which passeth all understanding, shall keep your hearts and minds through Christ Jesus.

PHILIPPIANS 4:6–7

WORSHIP

Almighty God, we worship You. You are the king above all nations. You are the sovereign ruler. You are the creator of the universe. And yet You love us, such finite and at times stubborn beings. You see us as we are. You see us as we can be. You love us either way, all ways and always. Our souls long for You. We would rather stand guard at the door of Your house than live in the midst of evil. What an amazing moment when everyone—everyone—will confess Jesus as Lord! We can hardly wait for that day. We worship You, Lord, our mighty God. There is no one like You. Amen.

481.

All the ends of the world shall remember and turn unto the LORD: and all the kindreds of the nations shall worship before thee. For the kingdom is the LORD's: and he is the governor among the nations.

PSALM 22:27–28

482.

My soul longeth, yea, even fainteth for the courts of the LORD: my heart and my flesh crieth out for the living God. . . . For a day in thy courts is better than a thousand. I had rather be a doorkeeper in the house of my God, than to dwell in the tents of wickedness.

PSALM 84:2, 10

483.

O come, let us worship and bow down: let us kneel before the LORD our maker. For he is our God; and we are the people of his pasture, and the sheep of his hand.

PSALM 95:6–7

484.

Look unto me, and be ye saved, all the ends of the earth: for I am God, and there is none else. I have sworn by myself, the word is gone out of my mouth in righteousness, and shall not return. That unto me every knee shall bow, every tongue shall swear.

ISAIAH 45:22–23

485.

And when they were come into the house, they saw the young child with Mary his mother, and fell down, and worshipped him: and when they had opened their treasures, they presented unto him gifts; gold, and frankincense, and myrrh.

MATTHEW 2:11

486.

And immediately Jesus stretched forth his hand, and caught him, and said unto him, O thou of little faith, wherefore didst thou doubt? And when they were come into the ship, the wind ceased. Then they that were in the ship came and worshipped him, saying, Of a truth thou art the Son of God.

MATTHEW 14:31–33

487.

God is a Spirit: and they that worship him must worship him in spirit and in truth.

JOHN 4:24

488.

Wherefore God also hath highly exalted him, and given him a name which is above every name: that at the name of Jesus every knee should bow, of things in heaven, and things in earth, and things under the earth; and that every tongue should confess that Jesus Christ is Lord, to the glory of God the Father.

PHILIPPIANS 2:9–11

489.

Who shall not fear thee, O Lord, and glorify thy name? for thou only art holy: for all nations shall come and worship before thee; for thy judgments are made manifest.

REVELATION 15:4

490.

And I fell at his feet to worship him. And he said unto me, See thou do it not: I am thy fellow servant, and of thy brethren that have the testimony of Jesus; worship God: for the testimony of Jesus is the spirit of prophecy.

REVELATION 19:10

ZEAL

How can we remain silent, Lord, when the forces of evil seek to silence us? How can we live according to our faith when the world tries to change us, confine us, defeat us? We cannot, must not, be silent. Your Word burns in our hearts. To deny our love for You would be certain death, whether physical or spiritual, mental or emotional. We cannot deny You. You are in every part of our lives. You call us to work while it is day and we have time. But when the night comes it will be too late. We must serve You with our whole hearts now while we have hope. We are Yours now and always. In Your dear name, amen.

491.

For he put on righteousness as a breastplate, and a helmet of salvation upon his head; and he put on the garments of vengeance for clothing, and was clad with zeal as a cloak.

ISAIAH 59:17

492.

Then I said, I will not make mention of him,
nor speak any more in his name. But his
word was in mine heart as a burning fire
shut up in my bones, and I was weary
with forbearing, and I could not stay.

JEREMIAH 20:9

493.

And his disciples remembered that
it was written, The zeal of thine
house hath eaten me up.

JOHN 2:17

494.

Jesus saith unto them, My meat is to do the will
of him that sent me, and to finish his work.

JOHN 4:34

495.

I must work the works of him that sent me,
while it is day: the night cometh,
when no man can work.

JOHN 9:4

496.

Be kindly affectioned one to another
with brotherly love; in honor preferring
one another; not slothful in business;
fervent in spirit; serving the Lord.

ROMANS 12:10–11

497.

Even so ye, forasmuch as ye are zealous
of spiritual gifts, seek that ye may excel
to the edifying of the church.

1 CORINTHIANS 14:12

498.

Wherefore I put thee in remembrance that thou stir up the gift of God, which is in thee by the putting on of my hands.

2 TIMOTHY 1:6

499.

Yea, I think it meet, as long as I am in this tabernacle, to stir you up by putting you in remembrance.

2 PETER 1:13

500.

As many as I love, I rebuke and chasten: be zealous therefore, and repent. Behold, I stand at the door, and knock: if any man hear my voice, and open the door, I will come in to him, and will sup with him, and he with me.

REVELATION 3:19–20